CAMPAIGN • 252

THE JEWISH REVOLT AD 66–74

SI SHEPPARD

ILLUSTRATED BY PETER DENNIS
Series editor Marcus Cowper

OSPREY PUBLISHING
Bloomsbury Publishing Plc

Kemp House, Chawley Park, Cumnor Hill, Oxford OX2 9PH, UK
29 Earlsfort Terrace, Dublin 2, Ireland
1385 Broadway, 5th Floor, New York, NY 10018, USA
Email: info@ospreypublishing.com
www.ospreypublishing.com

OSPREY is a trademark of Osprey Publishing Ltd

First published in Great Britain in 2013
Transferred to digital print in 2024

A catalogue record for this book is available from the British Library.

Print ISBN: 978 1 78096 183 5
ePDF: 978 1 78096 184 2
ePub: 978 1 78096 185 9

Editorial by Ilios Publishing Ltd, Oxford, UK (www.iliospublishing.com)
Index by Marie-Pierre Evans
Maps by www.bounford.com
3D bird's-eye view by The Black Spot
Battlescene illustrations by Peter Dennis
Typeset in Myriad Pro and Sabon
Originated by PDQ Media, Bungay, UK
Printed and bound in India by Replika Press Private Ltd.

MIX
Paper from
responsible sources
FSC
www.fsc.org   FSC® C016779

24 25 26 27 28   15 14 13 12 11 10 9 8

www.ospreypublishing.com
To find out more about our authors and books visit our website. Here
you will find extracts, author interviews, details of forthcoming events
and the option to sign-up for our newsletter.

DEDICATION

To Dore Sheppard – for always having my back.

AUTHOR'S NOTE

Special thanks to Rabbi Jeffrey Segelman at the Westchester Jewish Center.

ARTIST'S NOTE

Readers may care to note that the original paintings from which the colour
plates in this book were prepared are available for private sale. The
Publishers retain all reproduction copyright whatsoever. All enquiries
should be addressed to:

Peter Dennis, Fieldhead, The Park, Mansfield, Nottinghamshire,
NG18 2AT, UK
magie.h@ntlworld.com

The Publishers regret that they can enter into no correspondence upon
this matter.

THE WOODLAND TRUST

Osprey Publishing are supporting the Woodland Trust, the UK's leading
woodland conservation charity, by funding the dedication of trees.

CONTENTS

The Roman World, AD 54–74

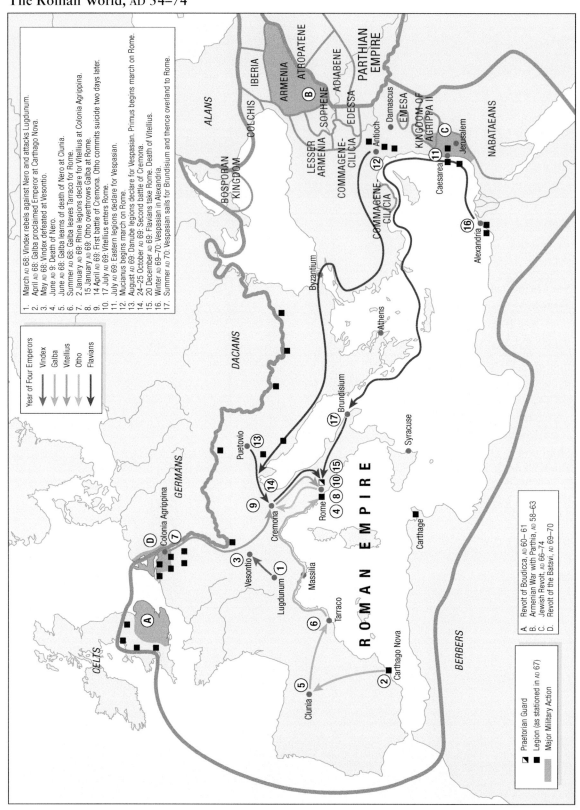

Year of Four Emperors
- Vindex
- Galba
- Vitellius
- Otho
- Flavians

1. March AD 68: Vindex rebels against Nero and attacks Lugdunum.
2. April AD 68: Galba proclaimed Emperor at Carthago Nova.
3. May AD 68: Vindex defeated at Vesontio.
4. June AD 9: Death of Nero.
5. June AD 68: Galba learns of death of Nero at Clunia.
6. Summer AD 68: Galba leaves Tarraco for Rome.
7. 2 January AD 69: Rhine legions declare for Vitellius at Colonia Agrippina.
8. 15 January AD 69: Otho overthrows Galba at Rome.
9. 14 April AD 69: First battle of Cremona. Otho commits suicide two days later.
10. 17 July AD 69: Vitellius enters Rome.
11. July AD 69: Eastern legions declare for Vespasian.
12. Mucianus begins march on Rome.
13. August AD 69: Danube legions declare for Vespasian. Primus begins march on Rome.
14. 24–25 October AD 69: Second battle of Cremona.
15. 20 December AD 69: Flavians take Rome. Death of Vitellius.
16. Winter AD 69–70: Vespasian in Alexandria.
17. Summer AD 70: Vespasian sails for Brundisium and thence overland to Rome.

A. Revolt of Boudicca, AD 60–61
B. Armenian War with Parthia, AD 58–63
C. Jewish Revolt, AD 66–74
D. Revolt of the Batavi, AD 69–70

◪ Praetorian Guard
◼ Legion (as stationed in AD 67)
▬ Major Military Action

INTRODUCTION

BACKGROUND

It was Pompey the Great who first involved Rome in Jewish affairs. Allowing himself to be drawn into a Jewish civil war between two rival claimants to the Hasmonean throne, in 63 BC he seized Jerusalem and profaned the Temple by entering the Holy of Holies.

After the emasculation of the Hasmonean dynasty, Judea was inexorably drawn into the nexus of intrigue and civil war that defined the terminal phase of the Roman Republic. It was hardly surprising that a Parthian invasion of Palestine in 40 BC, with the establishment of a Hasmonean king in Jerusalem under their protection, was greeted with enthusiasm by the Jews.

Rome's response – the intervention of the legions and, after yet another bloody siege of Jerusalem, the installation as a puppet-king, the half-Jew Herod in 37 BC – was deeply resented in Judea.

After Herod's death in 4 BC, the Emperor Augustus first divided Judea between three of his sons, then imposed direct Roman rule in AD 6. Herod the Great's grandson, Herod Agrippa I, reigned briefly over a reunited kingdom from AD 41 to 44. His son, Herod Agrippa II, was allocated a patchwork of territories to administer during the following decade.

Roman suzerainity over Judea was administered by a succession of procurators whose performance was as substandard as their credentials, and who lacked the military muscle to impose order. Imperial authority leaned heavily on local elites within the province, but these lacked the confidence or respect of the wider Jewish population. The result was endemic strife, with the line between bandit and revolutionary always a fine one.

THE LAND AND PEOPLE

The procuratorial Province of Judea consisted of the Sharon Plain along the coast, the hills of northern and western Galilee, the Jezreel Valley, the great upland massif of Samaria, Judea and Idumea, and the wastes of the Judean desert to the south-east.

The total land area of Judea was 9,650 sq. km. The northern region of Galilee is hilly and fertile, receiving abundant rainfall, while the south – the

Judean desert, Idumea, and Perea – is dry and rugged. A feature of the climate is the powerful hot and dry southerly wind called the khamsin, which can last two to three days or more.

Herod Agrippa II ruled a kingdom of scattered northern and eastern territories with part-Jewish populations. Another swathe of territory was controlled by the oligarchic governments of the Greek Decapolis (Ten Cities) immediately south of (and overlapping with) Agrippa II's territories in eastern Galilee and the Golan Heights.

The total population of Judea is unlikely to have exceeded one million. The city of Jerusalem itself is estimated to have housed around 80,000 people, although this would swell dramatically during the festival seasons. The population of the province was far from homogenous. It was fractured along ethnic, class and religious lines. Between the two areas of intensive Jewish settlement – Galilee and Judea proper – lay the territory of the Samaritans. Greeks dominated the cities of the coast and of the Decapolis to the east. To the south were the Idumeans, whom 'real' Jews looked down on as barbarous Arabs.

Even among the Jews proper there were intense differences over doctrine. Setting aside the ascetic Essenes, the chief fault line running through mainstream Judaism was between the Sadducees (who constituted the elite, the Temple priests, courtiers and great landowners who dominated the Sanhedrin, the Jewish Council of Elders) and the Pharisees, whose unadorned fundamentalism resonated among the common people. The loyalty of the peasantry, on whom fell the crushing burden of taxation required to both sustain the elite and meet its obligations to Rome, was deeply compromised, and Judea was perennially in turmoil. Would-be prophets, mystics and messiahs constantly sought to capitalize on the popular desire for some form of millenarian release; not just independence, but social justice and the restoration of the faith of a simpler time. This mounting frustration was reflected in the increasingly violent actions of extremist sects such as the Sicarii. Inspired by the revolutionary Menahem, their litany of assassinations terrorized Jerusalem in the years prior to AD 66, when all these tensions finally boiled over.

REVOLT

The spark that ignited this highly combustible tangle of class, ethnic and religious divisions was rioting that broke out in Caesarea when a Greek mob profaned the synagogue in May AD 66. The Roman procurator, Gessius Florus, chose this moment to collect overdue taxes from the Jews by ordering 17 talents confiscated 'for Caesar's needs' from the Temple treasury in Jerusalem. In response, some younger and bolder Jews took to walking about the city, railing on the procurator 'in the most opprobrious terms' and carrying an empty basket, begging spare change for poor, poverty-stricken Florus.

Incensed by this brazen insolence, the procurator marched on Jerusalem, took up residence at Herod's Palace, and demanded the Jewish leaders deliver up the pranksters. When the Sanhedrin pleaded this was impossible Florus responded by unleashing the troops under his command, ordering them to plunder the south-west quarter of the city and massacre anyone they found there. Jews who were Roman citizens of equestrian rank were brought before

The Judean Campaign, AD 66

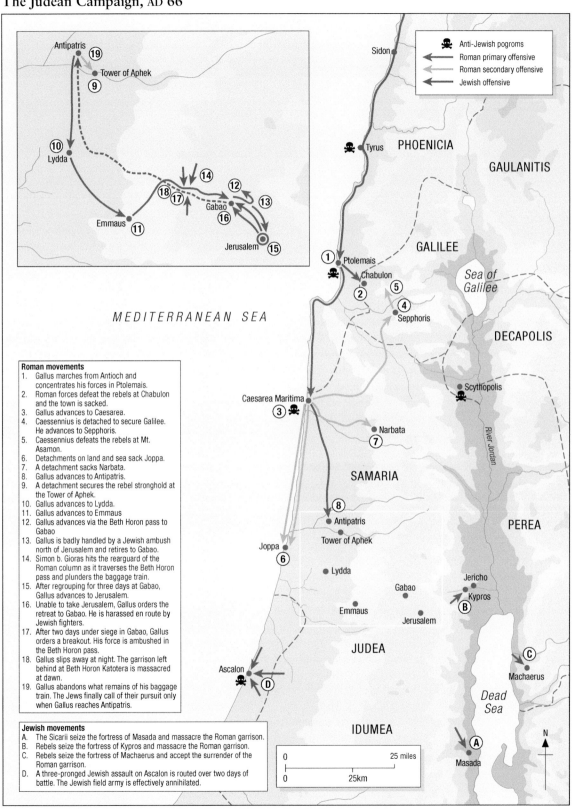

Roman movements

1. Gallus marches from Antioch and concentrates his forces in Ptolemais.
2. Roman forces defeat the rebels at Chabulon and the town is sacked.
3. Gallus advances to Caesarea.
4. Caessennius is detached to secure Galilee. He advances to Sepphoris.
5. Caessennius defeats the rebels at Mt. Asamon.
6. Detachments on land and sea sack Joppa.
7. A detachment sacks Narbata.
8. Gallus advances to Antipatris.
9. A detachment secures the rebel stronghold at the Tower of Aphek.
10. Gallus advances to Lydda.
11. Gallus advances to Emmaus
12. Gallus advances via the Beth Horon pass to Gabao
13. Gallus is badly handled by a Jewish ambush north of Jerusalem and retires to Gabao.
14. Simon b. Gioras hits the rearguard of the Roman column as it traverses the Beth Horon pass and plunders the baggage train.
15. After regrouping for three days at Gabao, Gallus advances to Jerusalem.
16. Unable to take Jerusalem, Gallus orders the retreat to Gabao. He is harassed en route by Jewish fighters.
17. After two days under siege in Gabao, Gallus orders a breakout. His force is ambushed in the Beth Horon pass.
18. Gallus slips away at night. The garrison left behind at Beth Horon Katotera is massacred at dawn.
19. Gallus abandons what remains of his baggage train. The Jews finally call of their pursuit only when Gallus reaches Antipatris.

Jewish movements

A. The Sicarii seize the fortress of Masada and massacre the Roman garrison.
B. Rebels seize the fortress of Kypros and massacre the Roman garrison.
C. Rebels seize the fortress of Machaerus and accept the surrender of the Roman garrison.
D. A three-pronged Jewish assault on Ascalon is routed over two days of battle. The Jewish field army is effectively annihilated.

Florus to be tried, scourged and crucified. Josephus says that about 3,600 people died on that day.

When Florus brought up an additional two cohorts from Caesarea the Jews blocked the narrow streets with improvised barricades and took up positions on the flat roofs; from here they pelted the troops with a hail of missiles, forcing them to take refuge in the Palace. The dissidents now seized control of the Temple and the Antonia fortress. Florus, utterly discredited, slunk out of the city, as did Agrippa II after his warning Rome would respond to such defiance 'by burning down your holy city and destroying your entire race' was met with abuse and a shower of stones.

The Jewish elite now split. A minority led by Eleazar b. Ananias, who held the post of Temple Captain in charge of administration and security, sided openly with the revolution and sought to seize control of it. Supported by the lesser priests and encouraged by the revolutionaries, Eleazar persuaded those who officiated in the Temple services to halt the making of the sacrifice that had been offered twice daily for 60 years for the well-being of the Emperor. It was, in effect, a repudiation of allegiance tantamount to rebellion.

The pro-compromise conservative majority group was led by Eleazar's father, former High Priest Ananias. The conservatives immediately attempted to get the imperial cult restored, and when their advice was rejected at a mass meeting held in the colonnaded Court of Women in front of the Temple, they began preparing a counter-revolutionary coup.

Secure in his own fiefdom, Agrippa II dispatched four *alae* of cavalry who enabled the conservatives to seize control of the Upper City on the western hill overlooking the Temple Mount and the Tyropoeon Valley, where the royal palaces and elite residences were located. The radicals still held the Lower City to the east and south, a predominantly plebeian residential district, as well as the Temple itself, which was now converted into a citadel. For seven days the two sides faced each other along improvised lines formed of walls, rooftops and street barricades. Several times Agrippa's professionals advanced in force and attempted to fight their way through to the Temple, but each time they were driven back.

Eleazar used the hiatus during the Feast of the Woodgathering to recruit reinforcements from outside the city, including Sicarii. He ordered the mansions of the wealthy, including Agrippa, burned, and then had the public archives destroyed, the latter targeted in order to win over the indebted rural poor and the proletariat. After the Antonia, which in determined hands could have held out for months, fell to the rebels after a siege of only two days, the conservatives were forced to either flee via underground vaults and conduits or take refuge with Agrippa's officers and their troops in the Palace, along with 500 Roman auxiliaries left behind by Florus.

It was at this point the chronic failure to synergize its various factions that so fatally characterized the Jewish revolt first became apparent. Menahem returned triumphant from Masada, where the Sicarii had overpowered and massacred the Roman garrison. His men were well equipped with captured weapons, and after entering Jerusalem 'like a veritable king,' in Josephus's scornful terms, he assumed leadership of the revolt and ordered Eleazar's father, Ananias, and uncle, Ezekias, executed.

When Menahem then entered the Temple to pay his devotions he was ambushed by Eleazar and his loyalists. The Sicarii in Jerusalem were annihilated; 'all who were caught were massacred', Josephus records. Menahem himself was 'dragged into the open, and after being subjected to all kinds of torture, put to death'. Some of the Sicarii were able to escape back to Masada, among them Menahem's relative Eleazar b. Yair, who assumed command there, but they would play no further role in the war.

Meanwhile, seeing no alternative, the Roman holdouts in the Palace sued for terms. It was agreed on oath their lives would be spared if they surrendered their weapons, but the moment they did so they were butchered on the spot. A wave of communal violence now surged through the entire region. Jews were massacred by Greek mobs in Caesarea, Ascalon, Scythopolis, Ptolemais and Tyre. In response, Jewish death squads ranged throughout the Decapolis, Galilee and along the coast. Tyre, Ptolemais, Gaba, Caesarea, Sebaste, Gaza, Anthodon and Ascalon were all subjected to Jewish retaliation.

By AD 66 the pass at Beth Horon was already the site of two famous Jewish victories; it was down this road that Joshua had routed the Amorites, and Judas Maccabaeus had defeated the Seleucids. The disastrous retreat in AD 66 was the greatest calamity the Roman army had suffered since AD 9, when Varus lost his legions, and his life, in the Teutoburg Wald in north-western Germany. (Bibleplaces.com)

This sestertius features the Emperor Nero himself leading from the front on horseback; an unlikely prospect, to say the least. But it does confirm cavalry in the pre-stirrup era could charge with lances couched. The backbone of the Roman army was the legion; however, it was the cavalry arm that gave Rome the edge in Judea. (Classical Numismatic Group, http://cngcoins.com/)

In the midst of this mayhem, the Jews showed some sound strategic sense. The last Roman strongholds in Judea and Perea were eliminated. Kypros, the massive bastion overlooking Jericho, was largely destroyed after its garrison was wiped out. The rebels took possession of Machaerus after the garrison was allowed to surrender. Such defiance could not be allowed to stand by Rome. The obligation to intervene in order to restore imperial authority fell to the governor of Syria, Cestius Gallus.

Gallus marshalled a considerable force of over 30,000 men at Antioch. At its core was *legio XII Fulminata*, plus 2,000 picked men from the other three Syrian legions, six more cohorts of infantry and four *alae* of cavalry, and over 14,000 auxiliaries furnished by Rome's eastern allies, including Agrippa II and two other client kings, Antiochus IV of Commagene and Sohaemus of Emesa, who led their forces (largely archers and cavalry) in person.

In September Gallus advanced to Ptolemais, where he placed the legate of *legio XII Fulminata*, Caessennius Gallus, in charge of operations in Galilee. Caessennius occupied Sepphoris without incident while the insurgent Jews fell back on the mountain stronghold of Asamon to the north-west, pursued by an *ala* of cavalry.

The clash at Asamon is instructive as it set the tone for much of the subsequent conflict. The lightly armoured Jews, using the cover of crannies and other natural obstacles, waited on higher ground to hit the heavily encumbered Romans in quick hit-and-run attacks as they struggled up the slope.

Caessennius quickly learned his lesson. While some Roman units kept the Jews pinned to their front, the greater part of the force was able to turn the Jews' flank and move up to higher ground in the enemy's rear. 'Being lightly armed, the Jews could not sustain the charge of the heavily armed legionaries', Josephus records. They were driven downhill, where the Roman cavalry was waiting for them on flat ground. The Romans lost 200 men in the encounter against about ten times that many Jews.

Meanwhile, Gallus led his main force down the coast from Caesarea via Antipatris to Lydda, detaching other units, by land and sea, to neutralize the rebel strongholds at Joppa, Narbata and the Tower of Aphek. With Galilee and the entire Judean coast in his hands, whatever token resistance he encountered brushed aside, and every village in his wake reduced to smouldering ruins, Gallus now assumed he could wrap up the campaign before the October rains rendered the roads impassable. Accordingly, the Romans now turned inland and marched on Jerusalem, taking the road via the plain at Emmaus as it twisted up into the hills through the gorge at Beth Horon. They bivouacked overnight at the citadel of Gabao, just over 10km north-west of Jerusalem.

Overconfident, Gallus neglected to reconnoitre his route the following morning. After breaking camp he allowed his baggage train with its

accompanying escort to lag behind, detached from the main body, while the vanguard of the Roman column walked right into an ambush. The Jewish fighters hit the Romans with such impetus 'they penetrated the enemy ranks, and with great slaughter broke through their midst', Josephus records. Simon b. Gioras simultaneously led an attack on the Roman baggage train where it was lumbering through the Beth Horon Pass that 'cut up a large part of the rearguard and carried off many of the pack animals'. The Romans suffered considerable losses: 515 killed (400 infantry, 115 cavalry) against 22 Jews and, portentously, forfeited many mules needed to transport the baggage and equipment.

None of the coins minted by the Jewish republic from AD 66 to 70 makes any reference to an individual. Instead, the coins identify place names on the reverse; 'Jerusalem' as on this silver coin and 'Zion' on the bronze coins. 'Israel' appears on the obverse of the silver coins. This marked the first occasion 'rebel' coinage was produced within the Roman Empire. (Classical Numismatic Group, http://cngcoins.com/)

Gallus was forced to withdraw and regroup at Gabao. He halted for three days in a defensive posture, with the Jews watching from the heights around. When he moved out the Jews backed off, refusing battle now the Romans were prepared, and the march was resumed.

Brushing aside Jewish skirmishers, Gallus set up camp on Mount Scopus, just over a kilometre to the north-east of Jerusalem. Convinced the Jews would come to their senses, Gallus did not press his attack. For three days he did no more than send out foraging parties to collect grain. Only then did he enter Jerusalem's outskirts. While the rebels withdrew behind the prepared defences of the Second Wall the Romans burned the suburb of the New City on the Bezetha Hill in a bid to dampen Jewish ardour.

Then, skirting the Antonia, Gallus established a new camp opposite Herod's Palace on the western side of the city. 'Had he, at that moment, decided to force his way through the walls he would have captured the city forthwith, and the war would have been over', Josephus claims. Indeed, there were collaborators inside the city willing to open the gates. Instead, Gallus probed the defences for a further six days before finally sending in a picked force headed by archers to attack the north wall of the Temple complex. The legionaries had just begun undermining the defences when Gallus, 'contrary to all expectation', suddenly abandoned offensive operations.

The unexpected setback at Beth Horon Pass with the loss of his baggage mules, the shortage of supplies necessary for the construction of siege towers and rams, and his lack of artillery or even scaling ladders all contributed to his decision. But the key factor was logistical; the imminent onset of the winter rains threatened to cut his supply lines back to the coast and retard his capacity to forage in the vicinity of the city. Gallus had assumed the Jews could be cowed into submission by the mere physical presence of the legions. But that gamble had failed. Withdrawing now would come at a terrible price to imperial prestige; but Gallus decided that option was preferable to being trapped between an enemy in possession of both the city walls and the surrounding hill country.

As Gallus withdrew his army to Mount Scopus the Jews fell on his rear. When the Romans continued their retreat the next day they were harassed at every step by the Jews, who hung upon their heels and poured missiles on

THE JEWISH TRAP CLOSES AT THE BETH HORON PASS (PP. 12–13)

Having abandoned his siege of Jerusalem in October AD 66, the Roman commander, Cestius Gallus, chose to withdraw west to winter quarters. On the fifth day of the retreat, the pass dropped steeply from upper Beth Horon to lower Beth Horon and was flanked by ridges and declivities (1).

The Jews flocking in from the farms and villages on all sides are lightly armed and undefended save for the occasional helmet or shield (2). A minority of these irregulars have bows (3); most are equipped with javelins (4) or slings (5). They keep the tightly compressed column beneath them subjected to an incessant barrage of missile weapons; according to Josephus, 'All along the route men were continually being struck, torn from the ranks, and dropping on the ground.'

As the road narrows the column is channelled into a constrained space. Some of the bolder and more heavily armed Jews are ranging closer to the enemy, seeking to pick off wounded or isolated legionaries, and help themselves to whatever they can plunder, especially Roman weapons and armour (6).

The cavalry was so often Rome's trump card when fighting on level ground, but this was not horse country. In the middle distance a small group of Roman cavalry are struggling to make the incline up the slippery rocks. Jewish fighters are giving way before them while their comrades pour missiles into the Roman flanks (7).

Each legionary was expected to hump his own pack while on the march, but now, stumbling over abandoned baggage (8) and their own dead (9) and wounded (10) comrades, most are too concerned with their immediate survival to continue shouldering this burden (11). Gallus had ordered all the draught animals slaughtered before dawn, except those bearing artillery and ammunition. This mule, bearing the tent, hand mills for grinding grain, and provisions for a *contubernium* of eight tent-mates, escaped that fate, but its longer-term prospects are not bright (12).

Towards the rear of the column, shrouded in the dust kicked up by so many thousands of pounding feet, the Jews have seized possession of the Roman artillery. Its acquisition would serve them well during Titus' siege operations four years later (13).

Many senior officers had already been lost; amidst the chaos around him a centurion continues barking orders to the men streaming by but without any noticeable effect (14). According to Josephus, only the intervention of night enabled the Romans to escape total annihilation. By the time it straggled back to safety *legio XII Fulminata*, in addition to losing 5,300 infantry and 480 cavalry, as well as all of its pack animals and artillery, had also lost its eagle to the Jews, a disgrace that would demand an imperial response (15).

The legionary in the foreground is advancing, shield drawn tight, *gladius* held low. His partner is covering them both from incoming missile fire, holding his *pilum* in reserve to throw or strike from the rear ranks. Relief on a Roman column from the praetorium of Mogontiacum (Mainz). (Erich Lessing/Art Resource, NY)

the flanks of the column. The legionaries could not respond effectively while in formation, and they refused to break ranks, because 'the Jews, as they saw, were light-armed and prepared to dash in among them. The result was that they suffered heavily, without any retaliation upon their foes.'

Having suffered significant casualties, a disproportionate number of whom were officers, including the legate of *legio VI Ferrata*, and the greater part of the baggage, the Romans struggled to regain their camp at Gabao. Gallus halted for two days while he assessed his options, but the delay only worsened his situation, as Jewish fighters were flocking in from all directions.

With the exception of those carrying the artillery and ammunition, Gallus ordered all the pack and draught animals slaughtered and then broke camp. At first the road passed through relatively open country and Roman cavalry sorties were able to keep the Jews at bay. But then the pass narrowed as it dropped steeply from Beth Horon Anotera (527m) to Beth Horon Katotera (378m), and was flanked by ridges and declivities that afford excellent cover and advantage to an attacking force.

Two legionaries at parade rest. Relief on a Roman column from the praetorium of Mogontiacum (Mainz). (Erich Lessing/Art Resource, NY)

Two Roman legionaries holding spears and shields. From the triumphal arch in Adamclisi, Romania, commemorating the Roman Empire's victory over the Dacians. (Vanni/Art Resource, NY)

When the Romans entered the pass they found themselves encircled and unable to operate tactically on such a narrow front. Compressed together, moving at a crawl, and under an incessant barrage of Jewish missile fire, Josephus says the entire army was 'indeed, within an ace of being captured, only the intervention of night enabled the Romans to find refuge' in Beth Horon Katotera. That evening the Jews occupied the surrounding heights in anticipation of resuming the battle at dawn.

However, the Romans secretly slipped away that same night. Gallus selected 400 men to take positions on the roofs of the village and call out the watchwords to give the Jews the impression he was still there while the rest of the army made its escape along the road in complete silence, travelling approximately 6km before daybreak. When the Jews realized the main force had escaped they wiped out the token garrison left behind before setting off in pursuit. Even after abandoning what remained of his baggage train it was not until he reached Antipatris before Gallus finally shook off the Jewish pursuit.

Over the course of the retreat the Romans lost 5,300 infantry and 480 cavalry, as well as all their pack animals, their artillery (which was to serve the Jews of Jerusalem well during Titus's siege operations four years later), and, the greatest disgrace of all, the eagle standard of the *legio XII Fulminata*. In addition, a Jewish leader, Eleazar b. Simon, captured the Roman pay chest, which he carried off in triumph to Jerusalem.

Gallus's punitive campaign had completely backfired. Instead of bringing the Jews to heel, his scorched-earth tactics had enraged them and his defeat had emboldened them. As Josephus observes, 'those who were bent on war were thereby still more elated, and having once defeated the Romans, hoped to continue victorious to the end'. Having succeeded only in legitimizing the rebel cause, by the time the remnants of Gallus's battered force staggered back into Syria almost all of Judea had slipped out of Roman control.

The fortunes of the revolt were now in the hands of the loose coalition forged during the siege of Jerusalem by the factions of Ananus b. Ananus, Eleazar b. Ananias and Jesus b. Gamalas. This government was dominated by the establishment of the priesthood and aristocracy. Whatever their prowess in battle, it had no place for the more radical antiestablishment leaders like Simon b. Gioras or, 'because of his tyrannical temperament', Eleazar b. Simon.

Ananus, a Sadducee and former High Priest, assumed the authority to mint coinage, appoint officials, allocate public funds and enforce the payment of taxes. He was careful to adopt the constitutional forms of theocratic government, listening to the advice of the Sanhedrin and having decisions ratified by the popular assembly that met in the Temple's forecourt. It was this body that divided the country into six military administrative districts – Idumea, Jericho, Perea, the West (consisting of Thamna, Lydda, Emmaus and Joppa), the Centre (consisting of Gophna and Aqraba), and Galilee – and appointed generals in command of each. This was not a responsibility taken lightly. The Jews had won the first round, but everyone knew the Romans would be back.

An inscription of *legio X Fretensis*, which served in Judea under Vespasian and Titus and then in the mopping-up afterwards, culminating in the siege of Masada. While *legiones V, XII* and *XV* returned to other stations in the east, *legio X Fretensis* would garrison Jerusalem until the first half of the 3rd century AD. (Author's Collection)

CHRONOLOGY

146–37 BC: Hasmonean Dynasty reigns in Judea.

37–4 BC: Herod the Great, Roman client king of Judea.

AD 6–8: Client-state of Judea dissolved and Roman province created.

AD 41–44: Herod Agrippa I, King of all Judea.

AD 44–46: Unrest as direct Roman rule reimposed over Judea.

AD 66
Mid–May: Anti-semitic riots in Caesarea. Florus enters Jerusalem in force; demands arrest of anti-Roman militants; defeat of Roman troops in street-fighting; Florus abandons Jerusalem to the rebels. Eleazar b. Ananias leads first aristocratic government.

Early August to early September: Factional conflict in Jerusalem; conservatives defeated; Ananias executed.

September–October: Sicarii driven out of Jerusalem; wave of communal violence and pogroms throughout Judea.

Mid–late October: Cestius Gallus advances into Judea; battle of Gabao; Roman attack on Jerusalem repulsed.

Early November: Battle of Beth Horon.

Mid–November: Ananus b. Ananus leads second aristocratic government; radicals and militias marginalized; Eleazar and Zealots confined to Temple Mount; Simon b. Gioras driven out; Josephus appointed military governor of Galilee.

Winter AD 66/67: Troops raised and strongpoints strengthened in Galilee; conflict between aristocrats and radicals; defeat of radicals in Tiberias; fall of Sepphoris.

AD 67
Early AD 67 to early AD 68: Guerrilla campaigns by Simon b. Gioras in Judea and Idumea.

Winter: Vespasian appointed to Judean command.

Early spring: Abortive Jewish attacks on Ascalon.

Spring: Vespasian's first campaign in Galilee.

Mid–May to early June: Siege of Jotapata; fall of Japha; massacre on Mount Gerizim; fall of Jotapata; capture and defection of Josephus.

Summer: Fall of Joppa.

Early September:	Vespasian's second campaign in Galilee; fall of Tiberias and Tarichaeae.	24–25 October:	Second battle of Cremona.
		21 December:	Vespasian, Emperor.
Late September to late October:	Siege and fall of Gamala.	**AD 70**	
		23 April:	Titus commences siege of Jerusalem.
Early autumn:	Fall of Mount Tabor.	7 May:	Titus breaches the Third Wall.
Late autumn:	Fall of Gischala, Jamnia and Azotus.	Mid–May:	Titus breaches the Second Wall.
Winter AD 67–68:	Overthrow of second aristocratic government by Zealot, Galilean and Idumean militias; John of Gischala, dominant in first radical government.	Late May:	Roman siege ramps against the Antonia Fortress destroyed by Jewish mines and sallies.
		June:	Romans construct wall of circumvallation and new siege ramps against the Antonia Fortress.
AD 68			
Spring to early summer:	Provincial revolts and downfall of Nero. Roman campaigns in Perea, Judea and Idumea; fall of Gadara, Bethennabris, Emmaus, Jericho and Qumran. Guerrilla campaigns by Simon b. Gioras in Judea and Idumea.	5 July:	Titus takes the Antonia Fortress.
		17 July:	Roman assault on the Temple Mount commences.
		27 July:	Jewish trap immolates the western colonnade of the Temple Mount.
9 June:	Galba, Emperor.	10 August:	Destruction of the Temple.
AD 69		20 August:	Siege of Herod's Palace commences.
15 January:	Otho, Emperor.	7 September:	Fall of Herod's Palace.
Spring–Early Summer:	Roman campaigns in Judea and Idumea; fall of Hebron. Overthrow of first radical government by alliance of conservatives and Simon b. Gioras, dominant in second radical government.	AD 71:	Vespasian and Titus celebrate joint Jewish War triumph; execution of Simon b. Gioras. Roman mopping up operations in Judea; fall of Herodium, Machaerus.
		AD 73:	Flavius Silva commences Siege of Masada.
14 April:	First battle of Cremona; suicide of Otho; Vitellius, Emperor.	AD 74:	Fall of Masada; end of First Jewish War.
July:	Legions in Egypt and Judea declare for Vespasian.		
August:	Danubian Legions declare for Vespasian; Antonius Primus marches on Rome.		

OPPOSING COMMANDERS

THE ROMANS

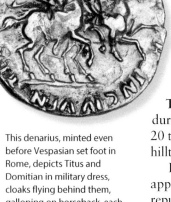

This denarius, minted even before Vespasian set foot in Rome, depicts Titus and Domitian in military dress, cloaks flying behind them, galloping on horseback, each holding a spear in his right hand. Vespasian was committed to the dynastic principle; as he told the Senate, 'either my sons will succeed me, or no-one will!' And indeed, Titus was the first son to directly succeed his father as Emperor. (American Numismatic Society)

The two men responsible for the successful reassertion of Roman authority in Judea were a father and son combination, one at the end of his military career, the other just entering maturity.

The Emperor Nero received word of events in Jerusalem while on a concert tour of Greece. It is representative of the reserve power of the Roman Empire – as well as a tribute to just how seriously news of the revolt was interpreted – that the total force committed to restoring order in Judea was larger than that used in the recent conquest of Britain.

Of undistinguished family and background, the chief claim to fame of **Titus Flavius Vespasian** was that he had served as legate of *legio II Augusta* during that campaign. Suetonius says he fought in 30 battles, captured 20 towns and conquered the Isle of Wight. His British experience in reducing hilltop forts would serve him well in Judea.

His subsequent career was uneventful. A term as *consul* in AD 51 and appointment as governor of Africa in AD 63 had not done much for his reputation or finances. By AD 66 he was reduced to serving as a courtier to the feckless young Nero, who very nearly ordered his execution after he dozed off during one of the Emperor's musical numbers; on the day after the concert he was refused admission to the imperial presence and banished from court. He was more or less in hiding in an out-of-the-way town in Achaia, fearing the worst, when messengers arrived with the news he was now Propraetorian Legate of the Army of Judea and in command of three legions – *V Macedonica*, *X Fretensis* and *XV Apollinaris*.

Why did Nero make this appointment? He needed a competent commander who could be sent to quell the insurrection at once, and so had to pick somebody from his own entourage. Vespasian looked like the best choice. Equally important, he was unlikely to threaten the Emperor's position. The same qualification influenced the two other appointments Nero made to eastern commands that would prove very significant for the course of Vespasian's career; Tiberius Julius Alexander as governor of Egypt and Gaius Licinius Mucianus as governor of Syria. The fact the former was an Alexandrian Jew and the latter a flamboyant homosexual speaks to the surprising degree of social mobility in imperial Rome.

Methodical rather than brilliant would be the best description of Vespasian's command style. Rather than go straight for the jugular at

Jerusalem he opted for the systematic reduction of the revolt in the outlying districts, employing a scorched earth policy of physical extermination to guarantee his lines of communication and supply throughout the province.

No patrician, the rugged and earthy Vespasian liked to lead from the front; as he reminded his men after the repulse at Gamala, 'it's my job to be the first into action and the last out'. This, plus his conservative strategy, the relaxed pace of the campaign and his propensity for indulging them in the pillage that was such an important supplement to their income, commanded the respect of his legions. When he departed to inherit the purple in Rome the legacy he bequeathed to his son was a smooth-running war machine and a clear path to Jerusalem.

Titus Flavius Vespasian, who began the war as legate of *legio XV Apollinaris* under his father's overall command, emerges as the near-Homeric hero of Josephus's history. He is always in the thick of the action; if there is an opportunity to make a decisive breakthrough, as at Tarichaea, or an urgent need to rally men on the brink of disaster, as happened frequently during the siege of Jerusalem, then Titus is there.

Although Josephus's portrait is hagiographic, there is no reason to assume this image is especially exaggerated. The portrait of Titus that emerges – an aggressive young member of the lesser nobility, anxious to carve out his place in the imperial system – is typical of the breed and the era.

Titus certainly understood the expectation of leading by example that was critical to establishing the bond between the officers and the rank and file. During the construction of the wall of circumvallation around Jerusalem he personally inspected progress several times a day. Once it was completed, he took the first night's watch himself; Tiberius Alexander took the second, and the third watch was shared out among the legates commanding the legions.

Josephus is at pains to emphasize that if Titus had any flaw it was his excessive compassion. At the conclusion of the Galilee campaign he declined an easy opportunity to storm Gischala because he was aware 'a general massacre of the population by his troops would ensue; he was already satiated by slaughter and pitied the masses … he therefore preferred to induce the town to capitulate'. His failure to establish a cordon around Gischala allowed John to escape and continue the fight from Jerusalem.

He made a similar error at the breach of the Second Wall: 'If he only had immediately knocked down a bigger section of the Second Wall or demolished every house inside the area captured, as he was entitled to do by the rules of war, he would have suffered no further casualties', Josephus comments. 'But he thought that if he showed himself reluctant to do the Jews any more harm when it was so obviously in his power, then they would be impressed' by his magnanimity. 'So he did not bother to widen the breach in a way that would allow his men to withdraw swiftly. He was under the illusion that people were going to repay him with equally decent behaviour if he treated them kindly.'

But a close reading of Josephus invites additional criticism of Titus's leadership. He was impetuous; his insistence on leading from the front led to his nearly being snared by a Jewish sortie on the first day of the siege. His tendency to underestimate the enemy led to his being caught off guard by another major sortie on the second day and forced to scramble to the rescue. It took too long for him to learn key lessons; he should have established his

wall of circumvallation at the start of the siege, not waited until two months of incessant Jewish sorties drove him to it. And on occasion he allowed his frustration to get the better of him, as when he ordered suicidal assaults against the breach in the Antonia and the Temple Mount. Nevertheless, Titus at the end of the day succeeded in finishing the project his father began. The fall of Jerusalem would be the cornerstone of the Flavian dynasty.

THE JEWS

The fractured prism of Jewish society makes defining conventional standards of command and control problematic, to say the least. There was a multiplicity of leaders throughout the period of the revolt, most with overlapping claims and conflicting imperatives.

By process of elimination, internally driven as well as by the confrontation with Rome, at the climax of the campaign – the siege of Jerusalem itself – responsibility for the defence had devolved upon two charismatic warlords.

What little we know of Yohannan b. Levi (better known as **John of Gischala**) was written by Josephus, the man who was to become the sworn enemy of 'this treacherous person… The most cunning and unscrupulous of all men who have ever gained notoriety by evil means.'

He was probably a small landowner, though he is often described as a merchant. Although it seems his origins may have been humble he did become a man of substance possibly through entrepreneurship in olive dealing.

At the outbreak of hostilities John was a loyalist; 'observing that some of the citizens were highly elated by the revolt from Rome,' Josephus says he 'tried to restrain them and urged them to maintain their allegiance'. His attitude only changed after the Romans encouraged the Greeks of Tyre and Gadara to despoil and burn Gischala. 'Incensed at this outrage, John armed his followers and made a determined attack on the aforesaid people and defeated them.' He then rebuilt his home town on a grander scale than before and fortified it with walls as a security for the future.

At first John was on good terms with Josephus, but the two later fell out and spent more time wrangling with each other for effective command in Galilee than they did coordinating a collective defence against the Roman threat. After the fall of Gischala, John escaped to Jerusalem and quickly inserted himself into the factional infighting there. A skilled intriguer, John was always more of an opportunist than an ideologue and ultimately had to settle for second place in the doomed city's political hierarchy.

Ironically, **Simon b. Gioras**, the man who bore ultimate responsibility for the defence of Jerusalem and the sanctity of the Temple, was half-Greek, his father having been a convert to the Jewish faith from the Decapolis city of Gerasa. Josephus describes him as 'A young man … perhaps not quite so cunning' as John of Gischala, 'but much fiercer and far more daring.' Most importantly, he was regarded with 'reverence and awe' by the men under his command.

Simon must have been with the revolt from the beginning. He first came to prominence with his successful attack on Gallus's rearguard during the Roman march on Jerusalem in AD 66. It is likely he led the insurgent forces to the north of Beth Horon, in the toparchy of Acrabatene, for in the following year it was from that region, 'which he had once commanded,' that he was expelled. The charge was banditry, but it is more likely his dismissal was part of the general purge of the younger and more radical fighters by the conservative junta in Jerusalem.

Simon refused to relinquish the area to its new general until compelled to do so by force. He withdrew with his men to Masada and then carved out a fiefdom of his own that came to rival the 'legitimate' rebel regime in Jerusalem. With the city spiralling out of control, he seized his chance when invited to restore order. With his uncompromised commitment to genuine Judean independence and popular appeal to the Jewish 'street' he was the natural choice for supreme command when the final confrontation with Rome ensued. His ultimate fate reflects Rome's perception that of all the foes they encountered during the campaign, he was the most ambitious, the most qualified, and the most dangerous.

OPPOSING ARMIES

THE ROMANS

Rome's victory in Judea was achieved by the *miles impeditus*, the fully laden soldier on the march, as much as it was by the *miles expeditus*, the unburdened soldier ready for combat.

The individual legionary had to hump a pack weighing 20kg, along with arms and armour weighing another 26kg. Nor was this the end of his burdens; distributed among his eight tent-mates (*contubernium*) were an axe, pick, basket, spade, rope, chain, saw and sickle; the mule bore the unit tent and hand mills for grinding grain for a total carrying capacity of 205kg, plus three days' worth of provisions; a second mule could bear a further 11 days' provisions, enough to keep the unit self sufficient for two weeks.

The humble mule thus emerges as the beast of burden by which the legions subdued the Mediterranean world. Mules had less carrying capacity than wagons, but boasted several advantages. They were able to travel both on and off prepared roads, and could travel further per day. In addition, pack animals take up less space both on the march and in camp, a major advantage from a military perspective. Accordingly, there were around 1,400 mules per 4,800-man legion, or one animal for each 3.4 men.

Meeting the subsistence needs of this four-legged transport pool could prove problematic; at a minimum, 100 hectares would be required to graze every 10,000 animals of the army train. As long as an army kept moving and sufficient pastureland was available, the animals of an army could, theoretically, be fed solely from grazing. But, since both green fodder and forage were more readily available at certain times of year than at others, the needs of animals are probably what made ancient warfare a seasonal activity.

Foraging for fodder – the *pabulatio* – is not how most people picture the life of the legionary. But it was a necessary part of the daily routine. A substantial proportion of the entire army spent each day devoted to foraging for foodstuffs – the *frumentatio*. Water was collected daily in the *aquatio*, wood for fuel in the *lignatio*, wood for building in the *material*; an army of 60,000 men would need between 24 and 30 metric tons of wood each day.

The Jewish revolt erupted about halfway through the reign of Vologases I, who succeeded to the Parthian throne in AD 51. Rome lived in dread of the Parthian composite bow, shown being strung on the reverse; the flat plains of Judea would have made good country for the Parthian horse archers. Vologases's decision against intervention doomed whatever chance the Jewish republic ever had. (Classical Numismatic Group, http://cngcoins.com/)

The daily supplies required by a 59-century legion amounted to 5.6 metric tons of grain and 3.7 metric tons of other foodstuffs for the men, and 4.6 metric tons of hard fodder and 9.4 metric tons of green fodder for the horses and pack animals. Even in the most bountiful of environments – which Judea was not – at some point the army would exhaust its capacity to live off the land and could no longer meet its own needs.

While resources might decline, the demand on the rank and file remained constant. The standard rate of march (*militaris gradus*) was 20 Roman miles (29.6km) in five hours; the forced march (*plenus gradus*) was 24 Roman miles (35.5km) over the same period. Beer and wine helped up the calorific intake to compensate for the rigours of life on the road and in camp. The basic wheat and salt rations were supplemented by cheese, oil, and fresh vegetables whenever possible.

But the fighting men did not generate the only pressure on local resources. Each legion was accompanied on campaign by a swarm of non-combatants, including the independent contractors and sutlers (*lixae*), merchants (*mercators*), camp followers (*ingenti lixarum*) and slaves (*calones*) 'who followed in great numbers,' Josephus remarks, 'and may properly be included as combatants,' for they yielded to none but their masters 'in skill and prowess'.

Accordingly, a smooth-running supply chain was a priority for any commander. The paramount need to ensure a continuity of supplies to the besieging force was one of the most pressing reasons behind Vespasian's order to improve the road from Ptolemais to Jotapata in AD 67 at the outset of his Galilean campaign. The best option was to move goods by sea. A month's supply of grain for an army of 60,000 would have weighed some 1,580 metric tons, and could have been transported in 26 ships of 60 tons capacity. It was important, therefore, to secure the sea communications between the strategic and operational bases. For this reason, both Gallus and Vespasian made eliminating the Jewish naval presence at Joppa a priority.

At the army level, responsibility for logistics (*commeatus*) was probably in the hands of the *praefectus castrorum* at headquarters (*praetorium*). This individual was responsible for the baggage train (*impedimenta*), including the army's funds (*pecunia publica*) and documents (*litterae publicae*). Closer to the action, supply depots and storage (*horrea*) were under the administration of the *dispensatores*.

At the climax of the Judean campaign, Titus was able to bring the following force to bear against Jerusalem:

Branch	Units	Unit Strength	Combat Strength	Non Combatants	Baggage	
					Horses	Animals
ROMAN						
Legions	4	5,190	20,760	5,190	920	6,100
Cohorts	10	810	8,100	2,000	100	2,700
	13	600	7,800	1,950	1,820	2,600
Alae	6	530	3,180	960	3,600	1590

ALLIES						
Infantry			11,000	2,750		3,600
Cavalry			4,000	1,200	4,000	2,120
Mercenaries			5,000	1,250		1,670
Staff			20	100	40	100
Train				340		1,360
TOTAL			59,860	15,670	10,480	21,920

The capacity to do so required standards of professionalism at all levels and stretching back far beyond the zone of combat. If the Roman beast of war had sharp teeth, it was only because of its long, long tail.

THE JEWS

Prior to AD 66 the Jews were a people without an army. The Jewish fighters won their independence in AD 66 through extraordinary efforts in extraordinary circumstances. Their innate toughness was never in question. Josephus observes the Roman apprehension 'the Jews possessed a fortitude of soul that could surmount faction, famine, war and such a host of calamities'. However, holding the land they had reclaimed presented a different series of challenges that ultimately could not be overcome.

According to Josephus, the 'most distinguished' Jewish fighters during the struggle at Beth Horon were Niger of Perea and Silas the Babylonian, seasoned defectors from Agrippa II's army, and Monobazus and Cenedaeus, princes of the royal house of Adiabene. Officers with experience, even in the service of foreigners, would have been prized for the professionalism they offered to an amateur army.

Nominally in command of the war effort, the real priority of the conservative junta was preserving the socio-religious status quo. Its policy was to enrol militia fighters willing to accept the authority of the military governors appointed in Jerusalem on their behalf into regular government units. Josephus gives us some idea how this worked when he describes the composition of the detachment sent by Jerusalem to Galilee. It consisted of 600 men who received three months' pay in advance, plus 3,000 civic troops (*politai*) and 100 regulars (*hoplitai*). This is a good example of how the new government tried to create a formal army in the hope the military balance would shift against the independent militias and thereby curtail the threat to property and power posed by the various bands of armed revolutionaries.

The traditional image of the Jewish fighters is of lightly armed men, favouring slings, bows, and javelins as missile weapons, and without armour, moving fast but, unless defending fortified positions, incapable of standing up to the massed weight of the legions. In the provinces this was undoubtedly the case.

In Jerusalem, however, the Jewish militias would have been better turned out. There were probably five sources of supply: the Herodian armouries raided at the beginning

Mars, the God of War, is depicted on the reverse of this sestertius minted by Aulus Vitellius Germanicus. The Emperor, however, 'the slave and chattel of luxury and gluttony' according to Tacitus, was the figurehead of the Rhine Legions, not their master. 'Seldom has the support of the army been gained by any man through honourable means to the degree that [Vitellius] won it through worthlessness', Tacitus concludes. (Classical Numismatic Group, http://cngcoins.com/)

of the war; the continuing output of Jewish workshops; arms-dealers; deserters; and the bodies of fallen enemies stripped on the battlefield. The fact so much equipment must have passed to Jewish ranks from this latter source helps account for the confused nature of the fighting that took place during the final, climactic battles on the Temple Mount.

One fundamental weakness in Jewish military doctrine remained constant throughout the campaign. The total absence of their own cavalry arm badly compromised the Jewish war effort, but the total failure to develop any viable response to the threat posed by the Roman cavalry fatally undermined it. Time and again, if the Romans could lure, or drive, the Jews onto level ground, they would be destroyed.

This fact was largely responsible for the critical turning point of the war, which occurred prior to Vespasian even setting foot in Judea. Still flushed with success after the repulse of Gallus, the junta in Jerusalem ordered a major expeditionary force to reduce the city of Ascalon, selected mainly because of its ancient hostility towards the Jews and recent pogroms against the Jewish population. The assault also made strategic sense, because the city fronted on the coast; it might have provided a base whereby the Jews could have been attacked from the rear while the main Roman effort was advancing from the north.

The significance of the mission is borne out by the fact the junta committed its entire mobile reserve – 20,000 men in total – under its most reliable commanders, John the Essene, Niger the Perean, and Silas the Babylonian.

The three-pronged assault was a well-planned and coordinated undertaking. The force headed by Niger of Perea attacked from the direction of Idumea, to the south-east. A second force under Silas the Babylonian attacked from the east, from the direction of Judea proper. John the Essene attacked from the north, from the localities neighbouring Joppa, where he had been assigned commander by the rebel government.

Ascalon was garrisoned by only a single cohort of infantry, possibly augmented by local auxilia, and an ala of cavalry – less than 1,000 men in total. But an exceptionally resourceful commander held the city. Known to history only as Antonius, he understood his advantages – discipline and mobility – and how to utilize them.

When the Jews assembled at Ascalon they rushed headlong at the city, but instead of sheltering behind its walls, Antonius drew up his horsemen on the flat plain outside. Then he charged. Undisciplined, badly armed, and on foot, the Jews did not stand a chance, as Josephus describes: 'When raw levies were confronted by veteran troops, infantry by cavalry, undisciplined individuals by regulars who fought as one, men with nondescript weapons by fully armed legionaries, men guided by passion

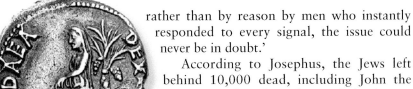

A 'Judea Capta' sestertius of Vespasian featuring a defeated Jew. Imperial propaganda highlighting the Judean campaign also ran to verse. The Flavian poet Valerius Flaccus praised Vespasian in the prologue to his *Argonautica* as being 'begrimed with the dust of Jerusalem, scattering fire-brand and causing havoc in every turret'. (Classical Numismatic Group, http://cngcoins.com/)

rather than by reason by men who instantly responded to every signal, the issue could never be in doubt.'

According to Josephus, the Jews left behind 10,000 dead, including John the Essene and Silas the Babylonian – distinguished commanders whose loss they could ill afford. Undiscouraged by the sight of so many fallen comrades scattered across the battlefield, the Jews made another attack the next day. Once again they were routed, sustaining an additional 8,000 casualties.

Niger, initially given up for lost when the Romans ran him to ground, eventually made his way back to rebel lines. But the miraculous survival of their last remaining commander was small compensation for the effective annihilation of the Jewish field army that, if Josephus's numbers can be believed, had suffered 90 per cent casualties over the two days of a failed campaign.

This disaster explains why the Jewish ruling clique did not furnish troops to Josephus in Galilee, despite his urgent appeals, but ordered him to muster whatever fighters he could assemble locally. Apart from the personal guard retained by each member of the rival factions, there was now hardly anything left in the way of a central reserve.

As a direct corollary of the debacle at Ascalon the initiative definitively, and permanently, passed from the Jews to the Romans. The defeat so chastened the rebels they fell back on an entirely reactive strategy of defending fortified positions, ignoring the lesson of Beth Horon that the only way to defeat the legions was by taking them off balance on the march in open country through difficult terrain. Instead of slowly losing a war of attrition against the Jewish guerrilla fighters, Vespasian and Titus were allowed to isolate and pick off their strongholds one by one.

The political implications of Ascalon were just as significant. The Jewish militia leaders lost faith in the capacity of the junta to prosecute the war; rather than integrate their personal retinues into a hierarchical entity under centralized control, they separately determined to retain their autonomy, hopelessly compromising any capacity for collective action and contributing to endemic factional infighting.

The result was a strange campaign, a war without battles. Ironically, by hunkering down behind the ramparts of their various citadels, up to and including Jerusalem, the Jews handed the Romans a fight on the very grounds they excelled – logistics, supply chains, and the methodical nature of siege warfare.

An aureus minted by Marcus Salvius Otho, with a stillborn appeal to Securitas. His three-month reign ended at his own hand after his defeat at the first battle of Cremona. (Classical Numismatic Group, http://cngcoins.com/)

OPPOSING PLANS

ROMAN PLANS

Rome's response to the revolt in Judea was no different from its approach to revolt anywhere within its aegis – to extract total submission from the affected territory by whatever means necessary. Grand strategy was the prerogative of the individual commander concerned; an established template of intimidation and terror dictated tactics.

Often, the mere threat of military action was enough to compel recalcitrant communities back into compliance with imperial authority.

A 'Judea Capta' sestertius of Vespasian. Here the Goddess of Victory herself looms over the despairing representation of Judea. (Classical Numismatic Group, http://cngcoins.com/)

The alternative was utter annihilation. Over the course of successive campaigns, Gallus, Vespasian and Titus all indulged the troops under their command in systematic murder, rape and plunder of the settlements and strongholds in rebel hands. According to Josephus, in one village after another along the legions' line of march, 'The able-bodied fled, the feeble perished, and everything left was consigned to the flames.'

However indiscriminate, this policy was method, not madness, justified as saving lives in the long term. In theory, once one community had been made an example of, the others would fall back into line more easily. In fact, no such domino effect could be applied to a culture defined by theocratic government and millenarian expectation. The ramifications for the civilian population upon the fall of Jerusalem were as grim as they were predictable. Josephus vividly depicts the legionaries as, 'Pouring into the alleys sword in hand they massacred without distinction all whom they met and burnt the houses with all those who had taken refuge within … running everyone through who fell in their way, they choked the alleys with corpses and deluged the whole city in blood.'

JEWISH PLANS

The total absence of any effective centralized government in the Jewish state makes any assumptions about a grand rebel strategy problematic. The goal was independence, but there was no agreement even about the form that

Although Vespasian had held high military, urban and provincial offices, he subsequently fell on hard times. By the eve of the Judean Revolt his finances were in such parlous shape he had entered the mule trade. The nickname *mulio* (mule driver) stuck. But the men under his command came to respect this earthy, hard-bitten commander as one of their own. (Classical Numismatic Group, http://cngcoins.com/)

would take – partial and qualified, as the realists were prepared to settle for, or complete and uncompromised, as the radicals demanded?

The shifting kaleidoscope of factional power in Jerusalem ultimately committed the revolution to total war against Rome, a war it could not win. The simple fact was a patchwork of urban militias and rural guerrillas could not hope to prevail against the unlimited resources available to an entire empire. But did they have to face this challenge alone? One factor that has not received significant scholarly attention to date is the role of international relations in the struggle for Judea. Did the rebels have a foreign policy?

Josephus states 'the Jews hoped that all their fellow-countrymen beyond the Euphrates would join them in revolt,' and in fact senior members of the royal family of Adiabene, recent converts to Judaism, did fight alongside the rebels; when Titus finally took Jerusalem he found among his captives 'sons and brothers' of King Izates. The support of émigré communities would have been welcome, but ultimately the survival of the nascent Jewish republic was entirely contingent on its capacity to find a great power ally to balance against the might of imperial Rome. The entire context for the Jewish confrontation with Rome, therefore, devolved upon deliberations in Ctesiphon, capital of the Parthian Empire.

Vespasian can hardly have been unaware his imperial ambition hinged on the security of the Empire's eastern frontier. In mapping out his march on Rome during a *consilium* he convened at Berytus in AD 69, one of the decisions taken, according to Tacitus, was the dispatch of an embassy to Armenia and Parthia that would secure his freedom of action without fear of interference from that quarter.

On this coin the mourning woman is accompanied by a Jewish man with hands tied behind his back. Vespasian had bound prisoners in this fashion and, to satisfy his scientific curiosity, thrown them into the Dead Sea to ascertain if they would float – which they did, 'as if impelled by a current of air', says Josephus. (Classical Numismatic Group, http://cngcoins.com/)

Vespasian had grounds for concern. Jewish relations with Persia had historically been very warm. It was Cyrus the Great who had freed the Jews from Babylonian captivity and, in marked contrast to subsequent Greek and Roman rule, Judea had enjoyed peace under Achaemenid administration. Vologases I, King of Parthia, would have been assured a warm welcome in Judea, and given the successive bloodlettings over the imperial succession that were draining Roman manpower, a better opportunity to once more extend the Persian frontier to the Mediterranean might never arise.

Yet, far from opting to intervene, Vologases instead chose to ingratiate himself with the Flavian regime. When news of the death of

Vitellius arrived in Ctesiphon, the king immediately dispatched representatives to Vespasian offering 40,000 cavalrymen to assist in the reduction of the Jewish revolt. After the fall of Jerusalem, Titus made a point of travelling to the historic point of contact between the two empires, Zeugma on the Euphrates, where he received a golden crown as a token of respect from Vologases.

What accounts for this policy of appeasement? Vologases may have been inhibited by the typical constraints on a Parthian monarch; the strategic vulnerability of the Empire's long northern and eastern frontiers (Josephus mentions incursions by the Dahae and Sacae nomads during this period); simmering provincial unrest (the king proved incapable of suppressing a revolt in the Caspian province of Hyrcania throughout his reign); and endemic dynastic strife (he had already been forced to suppress the usurpation of one son, Vardanes II).

The perspective of history and an understanding of the limitations inherent to the Parthian state probably played the key role in shaping Vologases' passivity. Twice before the Parthians had seized on opportune moments to strike deep into Rome's Asian territories – first in the wake of the Roman debacle at Carrhae in 53 BC, and then during the period of civil war subsequent to the assassination of Caesar in 44 BC. On both occasions local field commanders – first Cassius, then Ventidius – sent the invaders reeling back beyond the Euphrates. While more than capable of reactively defending its own heartland – as Crassus and Antony had found out to their cost – the loosely federated Parthian state lacked the wherewithal to go toe-to-toe proactively with its more centralized Roman rival. Recent events had confirmed this. Vologases himself had provoked a confrontation by installing his brother Tiridates as King of Armenia, a Roman client state. Parthian forces had acquitted themselves well during the ensuing war of AD 58–63, but the ultimate stalemate and brokered peace, even if it didn't exhaust Parthian resources, may have sated Parthian ambition.

If any of the factions nominally directing the Jewish war effort engaged in diplomacy or even had a foreign policy no record of it survives. Did they reach out to Parthia? There was no lack of precedent for a Jewish state forging alliances in order to counter the threat of invasion. Even the Maccabees had come to terms – ironically, with Rome – during the war of liberation against the Seleucids. The nature of factional politics and the ensuing lack of consensus within Jerusalem may have rendered diplomacy invalid as an option. The aristocratic government that held the reins of power during the first years of the revolution had very conservative goals. It sought

This denarius minted during Titus's brief reign as Emperor is interesting for its representation of a defeated and bound Jew, and behind him a trophy display of Jewish arms and armour, which must have been stripped from a well-equipped fighter serving in the inner circle of a militia leader. It includes helmet, cuirass, circular shield, a sword hanging from a baldric and two throwing spears. (Classical Numismatic Group, http://cngcoins.com/)

to hold the state together long enough to deliver it intact back under Roman suzerainty – with its own class restored to its accustomed role of serving as mediators between Roman sovereign and Jewish subject. Seeking an alliance with Parthia would conflict with this goal; it would only succeed in antagonizing their erstwhile masters and make reintegration into the Roman orbit a more protracted and costly process. Seizing control of the revolution in order to negotiate the terms of its surrender was one thing; but invoking Parthian intervention would amount to outright treason. That could culminate in a purge of the elite and more overt and intrusive Roman supervision of Jewish affairs.

Freed from any such inhibitions, it is possible that one or more of the radical militia leaders that battled for control of Jerusalem during the last two years of the republic could have appealed to Parthia for support. The appearance of rival delegations, each claiming to speak for the steadily shrinking slice of Judea still in Jewish hands, can hardly have inspired confidence in Ctesiphon, however.

It is equally possible that a combination of pride and messianic fervour stood in the way of any embassy. The rebels may have distrusted Parthian motives; having staked everything on full independence, why substitute a Parthian master for a Roman one? And of what merit was mere human initiative, anyway, when Jerusalem remained under the protection of the Lord? Had He not delivered the city from the Assyrians in 701 BC? In terms that no doubt echoed throughout the Second Temple many centuries later, He had pledged King Sennacherib 'shall not come into this city … For I will defend this city to save it for Mine own sake, and for My servant David's sake.' Reinforced by nothing more than a fatalistic commitment to the faith of their fathers, the rebels awaited their impending judgement alone.

THE CAMPAIGN

GALILEE

Joseph b. Matityahu – better known to history as Titus Flavius Josephus – was dispatched to Galilee by the authorities in Jerusalem in order to coordinate the disparate city militias under a centralized command. Bringing the local warlords to heel would have been challenge enough without the additional burden of some major cities, such as Sepphoris, being pro-Roman while others, such as Tiberias, were at best divided in their loyalties, on top of the ongoing ethnic strife between the Greek and Jewish populations.

Josephus established his headquarters at Cana, just north of Sepphoris. By leaning on the local municipalities for funds, Josephus was able to buy the loyalty of the local freedom fighters, guerrillas and bandits. A reasonable estimate of the total forces under Josephus's nominal control, including those operating more or less independently under allied chieftains, would be around 8,000–10,000. In addition to centralizing control over a field army, Josephus ordered the construction or improvement of fortifications at key sites.

Josephus appointed a council of 70 leading citizens as a mechanism for enhancing his administration, but the actual extent of his authority was extremely limited. While the pro-Roman element in Galilee considered his presence an impediment to the swift capitulation to imperial control they desired, the radicals demanded more assertive leadership and aggressive action beyond his derisory sparring with the forces of Agrippa II.

A persistent thorn in his side was Jesus b. Sapphias, the archon or chief magistrate of Tiberias, an advocate for the destitute Josephus describes contemptuously as 'a scoundrel who had a flair for throwing everything into confusion, and was unrivalled for stirring up sedition and revolution'. But Jesus had only provincial horizons; Josephus's great rival was John of Gischala, who sought not only to supersede Josephus's command in Galilee but ultimately to seize control of the revolution itself.

Josephus's own accounts relate one narrow escape after another from assassination in Tiberias, murder in Sepphoris and a lynch mob in Tarichaea. As if this wasn't enough, he constantly had to devise some new stratagem to outfox the repeated efforts to strip him of command by rival factions in Jerusalem.

Beyond keeping him alive, his guile enabled him to retain a tenuous control over the region. The Tiberians waited until Josephus had dispersed

The Judean Campaign, AD 67–68

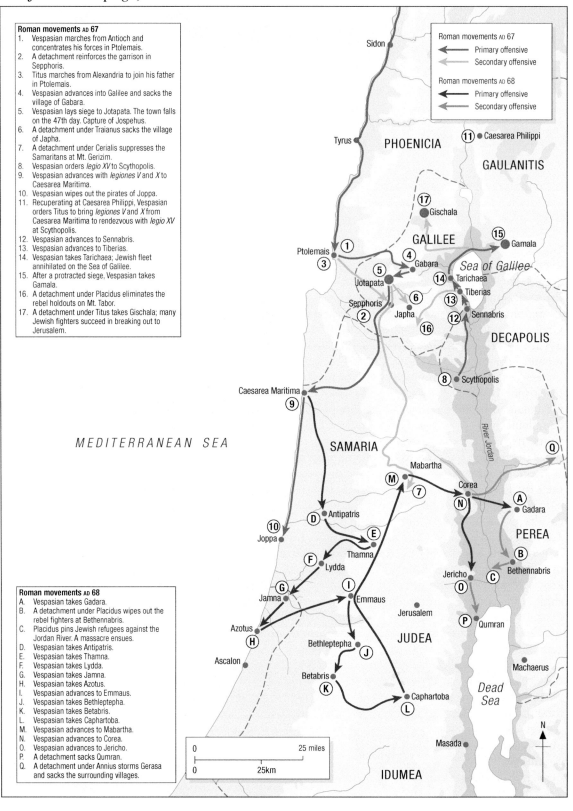

Roman movements AD 67
1. Vespasian marches from Antioch and concentrates his forces in Ptolemais.
2. A detachment reinforces the garrison in Sepphoris.
3. Titus marches from Alexandria to join his father in Ptolemais.
4. Vespasian advances into Galilee and sacks the village of Gabara.
5. Vespasian lays siege to Jotapata. The town falls on the 47th day. Capture of Jospehus.
6. A detachment under Traianus sacks the village of Japha.
7. A detachment under Cerialis suppresses the Samaritans at Mt. Gerizim.
8. Vespasian orders *legio XV* to Scythopolis.
9. Vespasian advances with *legiones V* and *X* to Caesarea Maritima.
10. Vespasian wipes out the pirates of Joppa.
11. Recuperating at Caesarea Philippi, Vespasian orders Titus to bring *legiones V* and *X* from Caesarea Maritima to rendezvous with *legio XV* at Scythopolis.
12. Vespasian advances to Sennabris.
13. Vespasian advances to Tiberias.
14. Vespasian takes Tarichaea; Jewish fleet annihilated on the Sea of Galilee.
15. After a protracted siege, Vespasian takes Gamala.
16. A detachment under Placidus eliminates the rebel holdouts on Mt. Tabor.
17. A detachment under Titus takes Gischala; many Jewish fighters succeed in breaking out to Jerusalem.

Roman movements AD 67
← Primary offensive
← Secondary offensive

Roman movements AD 68
← Primary offensive
← Secondary offensive

Roman movements AD 68
A. Vespasian takes Gadara.
B. A detachment under Placidus wipes out the rebel fighters at Bethennabris.
C. Placidus pins Jewish refugees against the Jordan River. A massacre ensues.
D. Vespasian takes Antipatris.
E. Vespasian takes Thamna.
F. Vespasian takes Lydda.
G. Vespasian takes Jamna.
H. Vespasian takes Azotus.
I. Vespasian advances to Emmaus.
J. Vespasian takes Bethleptepha.
K. Vespasian takes Betabris.
L. Vespasian takes Caphartoba.
M. Vespasian advances to Mabartha.
N. Vespasian advances to Corea.
O. Vespasian advances to Jericho.
P. A detachment sacks Qumran.
Q. A detachment under Annius storms Gerasa and sacks the surrounding villages.

Sidon

PHOENICIA

GAULANITIS

Tyrus

⑪ ● Caesarea Philippi

⑰ Gischala

GALILEE

⑮ Gamala

Ptolemais ①
③
④ Gabara
⑤
Jotapata
⑭ Tarichaea
Sea of Galilee

Sepphoris
⑥
⑬ Tiberias
②
Japha
⑯
⑫ Sennabris

DECAPOLIS

⑧ ● Scythopolis

Caesarea Maritima
⑨

MEDITERRANEAN SEA

SAMARIA

Mabartha

River Jordan

Ⓠ

Ⓜ
⑦
Corea
Ⓝ

Ⓐ
● Gadara

Ⓓ ● Antipatris

Ⓔ

PEREA

⑩
Joppa

Ⓑ

Ⓕ Lydda

Thamna

Jericho
Ⓒ Bethennabris

Ⓖ
Jamna
Ⓘ
Emmaus

Ⓞ

Azotus
Ⓗ

Jerusalem

Ⓟ Qumran

Ascalon

Bethleptepha
Ⓙ

JUDEA

Machaerus

Betabris
Ⓚ

● Caphartoba
Ⓛ

Dead Sea

N

Masada ●

0 _____ 25 miles
0 _____ 25km

IDUMEA

his troops to their home towns to gather in the grain and then defected to Agrippa II. Josephus responded by commandeering all 230 ships at the Tarichaean docks, put just enough sailors in each to navigate a vessel, and set off with seven bodyguards in his own ship. With this 'fleet' he sailed grandly down the Sea of Galilee to Tiberias.

When they arrived, Josephus had his vessels stand far enough offshore to maintain the illusion a powerful expeditionary force was packed on board. Playing this bluff to the hilt, he himself came ashore to accept the surrender of the city. Demanding hostages as a token of its submission, he had the city's elite – including the entire 600-man Tiberian senate – transported piecemeal back to Tarichaea.

But still Galilee chafed under Josephus's command. The citizens of Sepphoris appealed to Caessinnius Gallus, Legate of *legio XII Fulminata* and Cestius Gallus's deputy at Antioch, urging him to send them a Roman garrison. This duly arrived, and Josephus was unable to dislodge it. All Galilee was aware the Roman storm was gathering. Vespasian started from Greece as soon as he received his marching orders from Nero. Taking the overland route via the Hellespont and the Cilician Gates in Asia Minor, he arrived in Antioch where he picked up two legions, *V Macedonia* and *X Fretensis*, marching with them down to Ptolemais.

Sepphoris petitioned Vespasian to increase its garrison as Josephus's Galileans were preparing an all-out assault in anticipation of the Roman advance. Vespasian promptly dispatched 7,000 men, including 1,000 mounted troops, under Placidus, to reinforce the 6,000 men under Caessinnius.

Vespasian sent Titus directly to Alexandria by sea, where he was ordered to assume command of *legio XV Apollinaris* and march overland up to Ptolemais to join his father. When completely mustered, the legions were complemented by 23 auxiliary infantry cohorts (including the garrison of Judea, five units from Caesarea). Ten of these were likely *milliarae*, notionally twice the regular size. To this, Vespasian added six *alae* of auxiliary cavalry.

Regional client kings duly furnished their contingents, as per the terms of their rule. Agrippa II, Sohaemus of Emesa and Antiochus IV of Commagene each sent 2,000 foot-archers and 1,000 cavalry; Malichus II of Nabatea provided 1,000 horsemen and 5,000 infantry, largely archers. Not counting the servants, most of whom could also fight if the need arose, total army strength was not far short of Josephus's rounded figure of 60,000: three legions (6,120 men each); ten milliarae cohorts (1,000 each); 13 standard cohorts (720 each); six wings of cavalry (1,000 each); the auxiliaries of the Syrian kings (3 x 3,000) and the Nabataean auxiliaries (6,000) equalled a total of 58,720 men.

Vespasian also benefited from having an outstanding officer corps under his command. Among his subordinates, besides Titus, were Marcus Ulpius Traianus (father of the future emperor

Given Sepphoris was, in the words of Josephus, 'the largest city of Galilee, a fortress in an exceptionally strong position in the enemy's [i.e. Jewish] territory, and adapted to keep guard over the entire province', first Gallus and then Vespasian made a priority of securing the city by dispatching a garrison force to bolster its pro-Roman majority. (Bibleplaces.com)

The ruins of Jotapata, where Vespasian ran Josephus to ground. The site was heavily fortified and well provisioned for the siege but lacked wells or springs. To bluff the Romans into thinking the defenders had no shortage of water, Josephus ordered the garrison to do its laundry and hang the clothes out to dry on the city walls in full view of the besiegers. (Livius.org)

Trajan), who commanded *legio X Fretensis* and in ten years would be governor of Syria, and Sextus Vettulenus Cerialis, later legate of Moesia.

In May AD 67 Vespasian advanced from Ptolemais to the border of Galilee. His first objective was the village of Gabara, 8km from Jotapata. His intention was to send a clear message to all rebel-held territory as to the cost of defiance while expunging the disgrace of Cestius Gallus (who, according to Tacitus, was now dead, broken by shame and remorse). The Roman assault, taking no prisoners and razing the village, set the tone for the subsequent scorched earth campaign. All males of the neighbouring hamlets were subsequently slaughtered in view of their surviving families.

In the face of this onslaught the main Jewish field army, in camp at Garis a short distance from Sepphoris under Josephus's direct command, disintegrated as men deserted in droves for the safety of fortified strongpoints. Josephus left whatever men he could still trust at Garis and retired to Tiberias to contemplate his options. He sent a courier to Jerusalem demanding reinforcements sufficient to withstand Vespasian's imminent offensive, in the absence of which he requested permission to negotiate a truce and seek the best terms possible under the circumstances. If the council even deigned to reply to Josephus's entreaties no record of it survives.

JOTAPATA

The key to the defence of Galilee was the small, fortified town of Jotapata. It was located on the north-western edge of Lower Galilee, where it covered the heartland of the province against the approaching Roman army and formed the lynchpin of the ragged line of outposts strung out across the uplands. At the last moment, after the Romans had already commenced their blockade, Josephus slipped into the city to take personal command of its defence.

The initial Roman assault was checked in an unexpected sortie by the defenders. The Romans sustained 13 dead and many injured as they withdrew. The Jews suffered 17 dead and 600 wounded in this one action,

attesting to the doggedness of their defence. After a further five days of fruitless charge and countercharge Vespasian, who was wounded in the foot by a spent javelin at one point, which indicates he must have been standing dangerously close to the wall, recognized he could not take the city by storm. Jotapata had been built on a steep-sided ridge with deep ravines to the east, south and west, which precluded any attack from those directions. Vespasian ordered the erection of a siege platform against the wall on the town's northern side, and the construction of a battering ram.

In response, Josephus heightened the wall opposite the platform, added wooden towers and a new parapet, and stepped up sorties at night, raiding and burning the siege-works. When the ram was deployed the recently constructed wall began to crumble. However, the Jews rushed out from three different sally ports and, taking the enemy by surprise, set fire to the ram's protective superstructure with a mixture of bitumen, pitch and brimstone, which destroyed it.

The besiegers rebuilt the ram and toward evening started to batter the same section of wall. Josephus and his men fought throughout the night, sometimes sallying out to attack the team working the ram, although the fires they lit made them an easy mark for the enemy's artillery.

Toward morning the wall finally collapsed under the ram's ceaseless battering. Vespasian allowed his men a brief rest preparatory to the main assault at daybreak. Dismounting the pick of his heavily armoured cavalrymen, he stationed them three deep near the breaches, ready to go in as soon as the gangways were in position. Behind them, he placed his best foot soldiers. The rest of the horse remained mounted, in extended order further back, to cut down anyone trying to escape from the city once it had fallen. Still further back, he ranged the archers in a curved formation with bows at the ready, together with the slingers and the artillery. Other troops were ordered to take ladders and attack undamaged sectors of the wall, to draw off defenders from the breaches.

Realizing what was coming, Josephus placed the older men and walking wounded on the still intact portions of the wall and stationed his best men to cover the breach in groups of six (drawn by lot and including himself) to

The remnant of the north wall of Jotapata. Josephus built up the stretch opposite the Roman siege platform until it was 10m higher, using shelters covered in the hides of newly slaughtered oxen to protect his workmen against missiles. The moist skins gave but did not split when hit and were more or less fireproof. He also added wooden towers along the wall together with a new parapet. He used sacks filled with chaff as a buffer against the Roman battering ram, but the Romans pushed them aside with hooks on long poles. (Bibleplaces. com)

bear the brunt of the assault. He ordered them to plug their ears to avoid being frightened by the legionaries' war cry and to fall back during the preliminary rain of missiles, kneeling under their shields until the archers had used up their arrows, and then to run forward as soon as the Romans pushed their gangways over the rubble.

After giving orders for the women and children to be locked in their houses to stop them from unnerving their menfolk, Josephus took up his post in the breach. When the assault came, the garrison initially held their ground. They had no reserves, however, and under the inexorable pressure they began to fall back.

Anticipating this, Josephus ordered boiling oil to be poured down from the sections of wall that flanked the breach. Leaping and writhing in agony, the legionaries tumbled off the gangways, their close-fitting armour condemning them to an excruciating death. When the Jews ran out of oil, they threw a slippery substance – boiled fenugreek – on to the gangways, which made it hard for new waves of attackers to keep their balance, some falling over and being trodden to death. Early that evening Vespasian called off the assault.

Encouraged by the lack of Roman progress, the village of Japha, about 16km south of Jotapata, went over to the rebel cause. A detachment of 1,000 cavalry and 2,000 infantry under Traianus routed the rebels in the field; an additional 500 cavalry and 1,000 infantry under Titus arrived in time to participate in the siege and sack of the village.

Vespasian then had to deal with another ancillary threat. The Samaritans had no love for the Jews, but their loyalty to Rome was also in question, so when a large group of them began congregating on their holy mountain, Gerizim, in mid-July, there was cause for suspicion. Vespasian sent the commander of *legio V Macedonica*, Sextus Cerialis, with 3,000 foot and 600 horse, to lay siege to the heights. Tormented by thirst, the Samaritans surrendered their arms; Cerialis slaughtered many thousands to ensure there would be no further unrest from this quarter.

While these diversionary actions were taking place, Vespasian ordered the construction of three assault platforms at Jotapata, endowing each one with a fireproof, iron-plated siege tower. His archers, slingers and artillery were now able to bombard the defenders in comparative safety, and at close range, from the battlements of these towers.

On the 47th day of the siege the assault platforms overtopped the walls. A deserter informed Vespasian that the defenders, after weeks of struggle at the height of summer, were desperately short of water and had become too exhausted to put up

Mount Gerizim, the holy site of the Samaritans, who the Jews held in even lower esteem than the Idumeans: 'when the Jews are in adversity they deny that they are of kin with them, and then they confess the truth', Josephus maintains. Yet the Romans, taking no chances, surrounded the gathering on these heights and in one fell swoop effectively emasculated the nation. (Bibleplaces.com)

much of a fight. Armed with this knowledge, just before dawn Titus, a tribune, Domitius Sabinus, and a handful of men from *legio XV Apollinaris*, crept silently over the escarpments, slit the throats of the slumbering sentries and opened the gates for their comrades. Within moments the Romans had captured the citadel on the edge of the precipice, and as day broke they were sweeping down into the heart of Jotapata, catching its inhabitants completely unawares. The garrison was annihilated. The only prisoners taken were women and children, with one significant exception; Josephus himself, who was dragged out of hiding days after the town had fallen. By his own account, he was only spared because his gift (or bluff) of prophecy foretold Vespasian's ascension to the imperial throne. It is more likely the phlegmatic Roman commander was a lot more interested in his erstwhile opponent as a source of intelligence than visions of the future, and to spare his skin Josephus was equally prepared to play along.

JOPPA

At this point, Vespasian ordered *legio XV Apollinaris* to Scythopolis while he withdrew with *legiones V* and *X* to the coastal city of Caesarea. From here his next objective was the seaport of Joppa farther down the coast, which, despite having been sacked by Cestius, had been reborn as a nest of pirates. The settlers were refugees from towns and villages burned out by the Roman advance, predominantly fishermen and maritime traders from the Sea of Galilee, who now used Joppa as a base for buccaneering all along the Levantine coast in their commandeered fishing and merchant vessels. This menace had ramifications for the further maritime supply or reinforcement of the Roman expedition.

At Vespasian's approach, the pirates retreated to the safety of their ships. However, Joppa was not a natural harbour; the waterfront stretched in a

The Sea of Galilee, scene of the attempted Jewish breakout from Tarichaea. Josephus tells us that in the aftermath of the ensuing naval battle the water was 'all bloody, and full of dead bodies' while the beaches 'were thick with wrecks' and corpses, swollen in the hot sun, that 'corrupted the air' as they putrefied. (Author's Collection)

rough crescent framed on both ends by formidable rocky promontories, and when a violent storm blew up during the night, there was no safe haven in which to shelter and no escape from either drowning, being broken to pieces against the shore, or cut down by the Romans waiting on the beach. After razing Joppa to the ground, Vespasian left a detachment of cavalry in a fortified camp on the former acropolis, defended by a handful of infantry. The cavalry were given specific orders to ride out and devastate the surrounding countryside in a series of 'scorched earth' raids against the neighbouring communities, which they did every day over the ensuing month. The Romans had recovered control of the entire coastline.

TIBERIAS AND TARICHAEA

A fisherman's boat from the Sea of Galilee around the time of Christ, now at the Naval Museum, Haifa. It was in vessels such as this the Jews sought to escape from Tarichaea; in naval combat with the Romans they were outmatched, Josephus says, 'for their ships were small and fitted only for piracy'. (Author's Collection)

Vespasian then took time out for three weeks of recuperation at Agrippa II's estate in Caesarea Philippi. When news arrived that Tiberias and Tarichaea, both under Agrippa II's jurisdiction, were again up in arms, Vespasian ordered Titus to retrieve *legiones* V and X from Caesarea and meet him at Scythopolis, where *legio XV Apollinaris* was already quartered. Leading the three legions, Vespasian marched 32km northwards to the Sea of Galilee, and camped at Sennabris, some 6.5km south of Tiberias.

In the event, the rebels, under Jesus b. Sapphias, were in the minority; unable to hold the city they fled to Tarichaea. The pro-Roman citizens demolished a part of their walls as a symbol of submission to Vespasian, who entered Tiberias in triumph. He then brought his legions southwards along the western shore of the lake, setting up camp just short of Tarichaea, where Josephus had built and reinforced walls on three sides. The fourth side was fronted on the lake, where Jesus had established a fleet.

Titus, with a combined force of 600 foot and horse, and Traianus, with another 400 horse, were sent forward to probe the defences. The cavalry broke up Jewish sorties, inflicting heavy casualties and forcing the survivors to retreat behind the city walls. Titus subsequently ordered Antonius Silo with

2,000 archers to take the adjacent hilltop of Arbela, which was accomplished after a short, sharp fight. From that vantage, Roman archers could cover the city and sweep clear the walls.

Titus, seeing the waterfront approach was relatively unprotected, led a troop of horse across a shallow passage of the lake and bypassed the fortifications. Vespasian channelled more troops to follow up on this breakthrough and the defence collapsed. Some of Jesus's men were able to flee overland, but the majority retreated to the sanctuary of their boats on the lake. Vespasian ordered heavy rafts to be built and loaded them with infantry. This makeshift armada pursued the withdrawing Jewish naval force across the lake.

It might have appeared a mismatch, the Jews being experienced sailors on their home waters in familiar craft. But in fact, the boats of Jesus's fleet, being converted fishing vessels, were relatively small and fragile. The sturdy Roman rafts provided stable platforms for the missiles and coordinated lance thrusts that easily overwhelmed the unsteady rebel craft. Those rebels who attempted to board the Roman rafts had their hands and arms sliced off. Sword, javelin and arrow cut down the rest as they floundered in the water. No Jews survived the naval engagement. Tens of thousands of those who remained ashore were butchered or sold into slavery.

This coin minted by Vespasian bears the legend VICTORIA NAVALIS and features Victory standing on the prow of a warship holding a wreath and palm. It can only be a reference to the suppression of the Jewish rebels on the Sea of Galilee; even by the standards of imperial propaganda, elevating this one-sided massacre to the status of Ecnomus and Actium is a stretch. (American Numismatic Society)

GAMALA

News of the fall of Tarichaea brought about the capitulation of all of Galilee, with three notable exceptions: Gischala, Mount Tabor and Gamala. The last named was a strongly held fortress in the Jaulan, smack in the middle of Agrippa II's territory, about 19km to the east of the lake. It was perched on a spur of the Golan Heights that formed a steep-sided ridge shaped like a camel's back. The ground fell away precipitously into ravines on the northern and western sides, but sloped more gently on the southern side, and it was here that the settlement was built. The buildings ascended to the top of the northern ridge, the highest point of which was a rocky crag to the west, which could only be approached by scrambling over boulders, and from which there was a sheer drop on the far side; this served as the acropolis.

The only approach to the town was from the east, where the ridge of Gamala was connected by a sharply tilted saddle of land to the upland plateau of the Golan Heights. At the high northern end, where the defences ran up to the top of the ridge, a large round tower dominated the approach across the saddle. In addition, Josephus had further reinforced the natural defences by augmenting the walls, digging additional trenches and underground passages to enable reinforcements to be shifted clandestinely, and constructing a citadel atop the acropolis. Gamala also enclosed a fresh water spring – a critical deficiency at Jotapata. These formidable defences, under co-commanders Joseph and Chares, had easily held out against Agrippa II's rather half-hearted efforts to reclaim it for seven months, from spring to autumn AD 67.

LEFT
This aerial view of Gamala gives some indication of just how inaccessible the town was via the ravines on its northern and western flanks. (Bibleplaces.com)

RIGHT
The stone houses of Gamala were piled one above the other on a series of mini-terraces, creating the impression of a town that, as Josephus put it, 'seemed to be hung in air and on the point of tumbling on top of itself from its very steepness'. (Bibleplaces.com)

Upon receiving confirmation of the town's defiance, Vespasian interrupted his recuperation at the warm baths of Ammathus, just to the south of Tiberias, and marched his men to Gamala. Since circumvallation and blockade were impractical on such ground, and time was pressing, it now being late September and the end of the campaigning season, the town would have to be stormed.

Seeing the ridge of Gamala was, relatively speaking, the most practicable approach, Vespasian had his legions begin the construction of siege ramps at the eastern end of the town. He deployed *legio XV Apollinaris* on the north facing the tower, *V Macedonica* in the centre and *X Fretensis* to the south.

When battering rams succeeded in breaching the walls at three separate locations the Romans poured into the breaches and overwhelmed the defenders. But as the Jews withdrew, the Roman cohorts pursuing them lost cohesion as they were channelled into the narrow, constricted alleys in the upper tiers of the citadel. When the Jews rallied and counterattacked, isolated

Reconstructed Roman siege artillery, trained on Gamala. This is a smaller example; Josephus writes of a stone fired by a larger model tearing the head off a man standing near him and flinging it over 500m, and that when a pregnant woman was hit in the belly, the child in her womb was thrown 90m. (Bibleplaces.com)

Roman units suddenly found themselves being assailed from all sides. Many were cut down or crushed. Others sought to escape by climbing onto the roofs of the houses, which collapsed under their weight, setting off a domino effect as the buildings higher up crashed down upon the lower structures, collapsing them as well and filling the air with choking dust.

Many Romans were pinned down by Jewish fire from the heights; others became lost in the maze of alleyways and sinuous side streets; some, having completely lost their bearings and blinded by the dust, even attacked their own troops. Vespasian, who had entered the complex and set up a command post, was trying to coordinate the assault even as it disintegrated when he suddenly realized he was isolated and in danger of being surrounded. He ordered the few men with him into a *testudo* that held off the Jewish assault long enough for him to make good his retreat. Other holdouts went to ground as best they could; stragglers continued filtering back to camp throughout the night.

The breach from the inside. In the confusion after the failed first assault a centurion named Gallus and ten legionaries, trapped inside the walls, went to ground in a dwelling. While in hiding that evening the fugitives had to listen to the inhabitants boasting over their exploits. When night fell they crept out, slit the throats of the sleeping residents and escaped back to Roman lines. (Bibleplaces.com)

Roman casualties were heavy and Vespasian had to address his men sharply to prevent any demoralization. He also had to divert some of his force, 600 cavalry under Placidus, to deal with another rebel holdout at Mount Tabor, halfway between Scythopolis and the Plain of Esdraelon. Perched on its craggy peaks, the village was secure from assault, but the garrison, short of water and underestimating the small Roman detachment sent against them, unwisely decided on a sortie. Most were cut down on the open plain and the remnant surrendered.

The siege of Gamala arrived at its climax when, under cover of darkness, three soldiers from *XV Apollinaris* scurried unobserved to the base of one of the main towers and were able to excavate five massive foundation stones. The tower collapsed, panicking the sentries on the adjacent towers, who abandoned their posts, many being cut down as they fled. With both Joseph and Chares now dead a general panic swept the city, but the Romans, still wary after their previous experience with Jewish street fighters in urban hand-to-hand combat, held back until Titus, with a picked body of 200 cavalry and a small escort of infantry, led the way.

This time the Roman assault was more methodical; Jewish fighters, cut off from escaping to the heights, were driven back towards the walls and slaughtered. The remnant holding out in the citadel were stymied when a *khamsin* struck, sweeping dust into the eyes of the defenders and propelling Roman missiles upward. With the wind at their backs the Romans were able to seize the heights and exterminate the civilian population huddled there.

GISCHALA

In the wake of this hard-fought victory, Vespasian opted to go into winter quarters, ordering *legio X Fretensis* to Scythopolis while taking the other two legions with him to Caesarea. In order to stamp out the last dying embers of resistance in Galilee, Vespasian sent Titus with 1,000 mounted troops to Gischala, John b. Levi's home town. Titus offered the garrison peace with honour if they would submit. John professed acceptance of these terms, but begged Titus's forbearance for another 24 hours on the grounds the approaching Sabbath prevented observant Jews from either making war or negotiating peace. Titus agreed and, as a sign of good faith, withdrew his force to Cydassa, 3km south-east of Gischala.

That evening, John took his bodyguard and a sizeable number of fighters, as well as their families and some other non-combatants, and set out on the road to Jerusalem. At dawn, Titus took off in pursuit. Although the Romans managed to run down 6,000 men and round up 3,000 women and children as prisoners, many rebels, including John, were able to elude capture. Titus posted a garrison at Gischala and destroyed a section of the town's walls before leaving to winter with his father in Caesarea.

At the conclusion of a single campaigning season the rebel presence in Galilee, the richest province in Judea, had been entirely eliminated, and the Roman reputation for invincibility had been almost entirely restored.

JERUSALEM: THE RADICAL ASCENDANCY

The fall of Galilee discredited the aristocratic government in Jerusalem. Emboldened, the Zealots under Eleazar b. Simon and Zacharias b. Phalek seized the Temple and, to emphasize their defiance of the establishment, forced through the selection by lot of a puppet High Priest. In response, Ananus rallied the militias still loyal to him and to the other high-priestly families. They succeeded in penning up the Zealots within the Temple

The Haram Al-Sharif, the Dome of the Rock, as viewed from the Mount of Olives. Roman forces camped at this location in AD 70 would have enjoyed a similar perspective of the Temple. If nothing else, the surrounding hills would have enabled the Romans to keep the defence under close observation throughout the siege. (Author's Collection)

Mount. To achieve this they needed the support of John of Gischala, who had been received into Jerusalem as a returning general, the irregularity of his command being conveniently forgotten, a process no doubt facilitated by general regret at the traitor Josephus having been appointed to the post ahead of him.

But John betrayed Ananus by striking a deal with the beleaguered Eleazar. The two then sent delegates to the Idumeans soliciting their support on the grounds Ananus was preparing to betray Jerusalem to the Romans in order to perpetuate his own authority. The accusation was plausible both because some of Ananus' coalition, including Josephus, had taken that route and also because successful treachery at this stage in the rebellion would indeed have confirmed Ananus' ability to control the populace on the Empire's behalf, which was precisely the quality desired by Rome in selecting the provincials through whom she ruled. Just as important for the Idumeans was the need to find competent generals to replace Ananus' colleagues in the fight against Rome. The problem was urgent for them, for after what had happened in Galilee they anticipated a Roman assault on their territory when the next campaigning season opened.

The Idumeans marched on Jerusalem and, aided by the Zealots, who had slipped out of the Temple and opened the gates under cover of a storm, seized control of the city. Ananus' faction was purged, beginning with Ananus himself. The more radical regime that emerged from violence of this transition could have legitimized itself had it offered much-needed stability, but the coalition of John, Eleazar and the Idumeans proved even less cohesive than its predecessor. Some of the Idumeans under Jacob b. Sosias, who was dissatisfied with his junior partner status, liberated about 2,000 citizens from the prisons and defected to Simon b. Gioras out in the Judean countryside.

Since being purged by the aristocratic regime, Simon had overrun the toparchy of Acrabatene and the surrounding region as far south as Idumea, drilling his followers until he 'no longer had a mob of slaves and robbers, but an army of soldiers who obeyed him as if he were their king,' Josephus remarks.

Alarmed, John and Eleazar launched a pre-emptive assault against Simon; its failure, unlike the expedition by Ananus' generals nearly two years before, testifies to Simon's growing power, as does his campaign through Idumea, where 'nothing save desert remained in the wake of Simon's army,' Josephus comments. Simon moved on Jerusalem in the spring of AD 69 and encamped outside its walls. John and Eleazar were reduced to kidnapping his wife in the hope he would lay down his arms to ransom her. Even more pathetically, they returned her to him to placate his fury. This display of weakness convinced those Idumeans who had remained in Jerusalem to turn on John and Eleazar, ironically forcing them to take refuge in the Temple from which the Idumean intervention had originally rescued them.

A three-cornered struggle, as impious as it was futile, then ensued between Eleazar, who had seized the inner court of the Temple, including the Holy of Holies; John, who controlled the outer court and the porticoes that encircled the Temple Mount; and Simon, who was master of the city. Eleazar sought to break this impasse by coming to terms with Simon, but was pre-empted by John, who smuggled armed men into the Temple under the pretext of attending Passover. These seized control of the inner court; Eleazar was forced to surrender control of his militias and swear fealty to John. Only the arrival of the Romans brought an end to this endemic factional infighting, the sole accomplishment of which was the burning of the storehouses where large quantities of grain had been laid aside in preparation for the impending siege. This was to have appalling consequences.

The view over the Old City of Jerusalem from the Citadel. The Dome of the Rock is in the middle distance; to the west, the bell tower of the Church of the Ascension dominates the peak of the Mount of Olives, the site of the camp of *legio X Fretensis* in AD 66. (Author's Collection)

THE YEAR OF THE FOUR EMPERORS

As the campaign season of AD 68 opened the Romans, observing affairs in Jerusalem with a wry detachment, were in no hurry to intervene. 'God is a much better general than I am,' Vespasian informed his men, 'and, by the way he is handing over the Jews to the Romans without any effort on our part, he is giving our army a bloodless victory. Since our enemies are busy dying by their own hands,' he concluded, the best option in the circumstances 'is to stay as spectators instead of taking on fanatics who welcome death and are already busy murdering each other.'

A peripheral strategy was appropriate, and the first objective was the rugged, mountainous province of Perea east of Galilee. Crossing the Jordan, the Romans advanced on Perea's capital, Gadara, where the populace expelled their Zealot garrison and surrendered the city. Vespasian sent Placidus with a force of 3,000 infantry and 500 horse in pursuit of the fleeing Zealots, who took refuge in a large fortified village called Bethennabris. Most of the rebels were slaughtered on open ground during a sortie, the rest after the Romans stormed the village that evening.

Terrified, the region's entire population fled towards Jericho, but their escape was thwarted by the Jordan River, swollen by rain and no longer fordable. Placidus descended on the fugitives pinned against the riverbank, massacring 15,000 while 'an incalculable number' threw themselves into the Jordan and drowned. In addition to whatever captives they allowed to live, the Romans seized countless donkeys, sheep, oxen, camels and other worldly goods. Exploiting the general terror, Placidus quickly moved to pacify all of Perea. In short order the only toehold remaining to the Jews east of the Dead Sea was the fortress of Machaerus.

Leaving Traianus in overall command of the operation, Vespasian meanwhile marched back to Caesarea and inland down to Antipatris, where he restored Roman rule. After this, he devastated a wide circle of the surrounding region 'with fire and sword', destroying every village as he went. Having conquered the territory around Thamna, he overpowered the rebel garrisons at Jama, Azotus and Lydda in order to ensure Roman freedom of movement along the coast road – an important consideration for the forthcoming siege of Jerusalem – effectively purging any lingering defiance on the Plain of Sharon.

Advancing to Emmaus, where he left *legio V Macedonica* in order to block the approaches to Jerusalem, Vespasian moved on to Bethleptepha south-west of the capital, burning it to the ground and laying waste the surrounding countryside. Marching even further south, across the Judean border into Idumea, he captured two important villages, Betabris and Caphartoba, putting 10,000 of their inhabitants to the sword and enslaving another thousand. He then circled back north

The bullet-pocked Zion Gate still bears the scars of a more recent war of independence. This is where Israeli forces broke through to the Old City in 1948. The gates that confronted Titus would have been of a similar design; going over, or through, the walls was the preferred option. (Author's Collection)

through the hills to Jericho, most of whose inhabitants fled into the surrounding mountains at the first sign of his approach.

Vespasian was soon joined by Traianus and Placidus, reinforcements that enabled him to establish fortified camps at Jericho and Adida. In addition, he sent Lucius Annius to the city of Gerasa with a small mixed force of horse and infantry. Annius stormed it at his first attempt, massacring the garrison, enslaving the rest of the population and then, after allowing his soldiers to loot the houses, setting fire to the city – a process he repeated at all the surrounding villages.

The campaign season of AD 69 began on a similar note. Dispatching Sextus Cerialis to complete the reduction of Idumea, Vespasian marched on Jerusalem from the north. He established garrisons in the towns that anchored his supply lines back to the coast, while his cavalry stamped out whatever resistance remained in the immediate environment of the holy city.

The noose was tightening; only a miracle could save Jerusalem now. And it was precisely at this moment the miracle of deliverance transpired, not in Judea but at the opposite end of the Roman Empire.

Discontent with Nero's personal and fiscal excesses had been building for some time. Reprisals for alleged or real conspiracies against the Emperor had already cost such prominent statesmen as Lucan, Seneca and Corbulo their lives.

Provincial unrest finally boiled over in March AD 68 when Gaius Julius Vindex, the governor of Gallia Lugdunensis declared against Nero. His revolt was crushed two months later, but in the meantime Servius Sulpicius Galba, the governor of Hispania Tarraconensis, had also declared his independence and, with nothing to lose, was marching, this time unhindered, on Rome. Deserted by the Praetorian Guard, Nero was hounded into committing suicide on 9 June.

The polite fiction that had disguised the autocracy of the Principate was exposed, 'for now had been divulged that secret of the empire, that emperors could be made elsewhere than at Rome,' Tacitus noted. Galba was usurped in short order by Marcus Salvius Otho, and Otho in turn by Aulus Vitellius Germanicus.

The anarchy in Rome during this Year of the Four Emperors encouraged spiralling defiance of imperial authority in the provinces. Lucius Clodius Macer, governor of Africa, revolted in May AD 68, cutting off grain shipments to Rome until his assassination in October AD 68. The governor of the two Mauretanian provinces was murdered, the governors of Corsica and Britain driven out, in the latter instance a tribal people, the Brigantes, seizing on the opportunity to throw off their allegiance to Rome.

Most seriously, the Batavians rose in a revolt under Gaius Julius Civilis that culminated in the annihilation of two legions (I *Germanica* and *XV Primigenia*) and the defection of two more (I *Germanica* and *XVI Gallica*). When Belgica declared for the rebels many feared a domino effect could lead to all Gaul detaching itself from the Empire.

With the Empire consuming itself at its core and hard pressed on its frontiers, the campaign in Judea ground to a halt as Vespasian paused, first to wait until the situation stabilized, then to consider his own options. His decision to bid for the imperial throne was publicly staged in Alexandria on 1 July AD 69. In front of the legions roaring their approval, he was proclaimed Caesar by the prefect of Egypt, Tiberius Alexander.

The Judean Campaign, AD 69–70

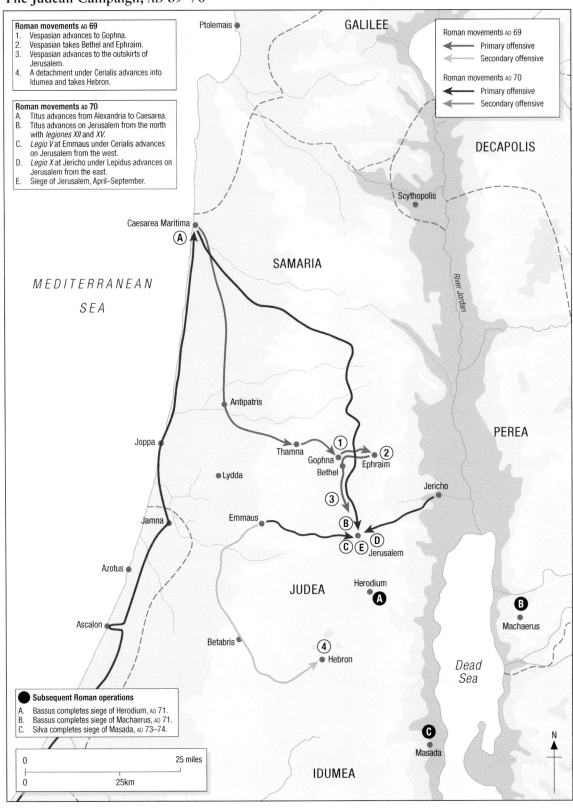

Roman movements AD 69
1. Vespasian advances to Gophna.
2. Vespasian takes Bethel and Ephraim.
3. Vespasian advances to the outskirts of Jerusalem.
4. A detachment under Cerialis advances into Idumea and takes Hebron.

Roman movements AD 70
A. Titus advances from Alexandria to Caesarea.
B. Titus advances on Jerusalem from the north with *legiones XII* and *XV*.
C. *Legio V* at Emmaus under Cerialis advances on Jerusalem from the west.
D. *Legio X* at Jericho under Lepidus advances on Jerusalem from the east.
E. Siege of Jerusalem, April–September.

Roman movements AD 69
← Primary offensive
← Secondary offensive

Roman movements AD 70
← Primary offensive
← Secondary offensive

● **Subsequent Roman operations**
A. Bassus completes siege of Herodium, AD 71.
B. Bassus completes siege of Machaerus, AD 71.
C. Silva completes siege of Masada, AD 73–74.

GALILEE

Ptolemais

DECAPOLIS

Scythopolis

Caesarea Maritima
Ⓐ

SAMARIA

MEDITERRANEAN
SEA

River Jordan

PEREA

Antipatris

Joppa

Thamna

Gophna ①

② Ephraim

Bethel

Lydda

③

Jericho

Jamna

Emmaus

Ⓑ

Ⓒ Ⓔ Ⓓ
Jerusalem

Azotus

JUDEA

Herodium
Ⓐ

Ⓑ
Machaerus

Ascalon

Betabris

④
Hebron

Dead Sea

Ⓒ
Masada

IDUMEA

0 ——————— 25 miles
0 ——————— 25km

N ↑

50

At a council of war held in Berytus it was determined Vespasian would establish Flavian headquarters in Egypt. Tiberius would serve with Titus in the consummation of the Judean campaign, while Mucianus would take the fight to Vitellius in Italy.

Mucianus was given a relatively small force, one entire legion from Syria (*VI Ferrata*) and detachments of 2,600 men apiece from the other five legions operating there and in Judea, for a total of approximately 18,000 legionaries. The Flavians anticipated he would be joined by the legions stationed in Moesia, Pannonia and Dalmatia as he advanced through the Balkans, and then from the dissident ex-Othonian praetorians who had been dispersed about northern Italy by Vitellius.

This strategy actually unfolded ahead of schedule. Even before Mucianus crossed the Bosphorus, Antonius Primus, commander of *legio VI Ferrata* in Pannonia, and Cornelius Fuscus, the imperial procurator in Illyricum, led the five legions on the Danube in a rapid descent on Italy, defeating the Vitellians in a battle at Cremona. The legions in Spain, Gaul and Britain now swore allegiance to Vespasian, who pondered refining the plan decided on in Berytus by invading the province of Africa and cutting off its shipments of grain to Rome, but his plans were overtaken by events.

On 18 December Vespasian's brother, Titus Flavius Sabinus, the prefect of the urban cohorts at Rome, made a premature bid for power. Rebuffed, he seized the peak of the Capitol with a motley assortment of soldiers, senators, and knights. The Vitellians burnt them out the following day; Sabinus was decapitated and his headless trunk dragged through the streets. But it was all futile; Mucianus was at the gates. Vitellius, utterly forsaken and reduced to propping a couch and mattress against the palace door, was hauled to the Forum, tortured, murdered and dumped in the Tiber. The way was now clear; even as the struggle for Jerusalem reached its climax in the summer of AD 70, Vespasian set sail from Alexandria to claim his prize.

JERUSALEM: INVESTITURE

Titus began the Jerusalem campaign in the spring of that year. Departing Alexandria the Romans marched to Raphia, which marked the Judean border, then on to Gaza. Continuing along the coast by way of Ascalon, Jamna and Joppa, they proceeded to Caesarea.

The army that assembled there was larger than that commanded by Vespasian. At its core were four legions; *XV Apollinaris*, which Titus had brought from Alexandria at the beginning of the war, commanded by Titus Frigius; *V Macedonica*, which Vespasian had stationed at Emmaus, commanded by Sextus Cerialis; *X Fretensis*, which Vespasian had stationed at Jericho, commanded by Larcius Lepidus; and *XII Fulminata*. Josephus does not name its commander, but he and the men under him were doubtless keen to avenge their disgraceful rout by the Jews in AD 66. These legions had been depleted to flesh out the army that Mucianus led through Asia Minor to confront Vitellius, but they were now brought back up to full strength, partly from the detachments that Titus brought from Egypt and partly from forts on the Euphrates.

Supporting the legions were 20 cohorts of auxiliary infantry and eight alae of cavalry. In addition, there were substantial detachments of local

The modern towers of David and Hippicus, from an Ottoman-era postcard of Jerusalem. The Tower of David was based upon the Phasael Tower, named after Herod the Great's brother, the largest of the three established by Herod to guard the main gate to the city. (Bibleplaces.com)

troops that had been provided by the region's client rulers. These were led in person by King Agrippa II and King Sohaemus of Emesa, and included, according to Tacitus, 'strong levies of Arabs, who felt for the Jews the hatred common between neighbours, and many individual adventurers from Rome and Italy, who for various reasons hoped to ingratiate themselves with an emperor whose ear might be gained'. The constraints of security and supply in the Judean hill country prevented Titus from marching the main force in a single column. Instead he sent *V Macedonica* via Emmaus and *X Fretensis* via Jericho, taking *legiones XII* and *XV* with him on the direct road to Jerusalem.

However they arrived, it was 23 April when the lead units of *legiones XV* and *XII* appeared on the hills north of the city. During the night *legio V Macedonica* arrived, and the next morning Titus, as Gallus had before him, moved his army up onto Mount Scopus, the famous vantage point from where pilgrims traditionally caught their first sight of the great city and the gleaming white and gold Sanctuary of the Temple.

The magnitude of the task before them must have been immediately apparent. According to Tacitus:

> Standing on a height which is naturally difficult of access, Jerusalem was rendered even more impregnable by ramparts and bastions that would have made even places on a flat plain more than adequately fortified. Two very high hills were surrounded by walls that in some places jutted out but in others curved in, so that the flanks of any besiegers were exposed to enemy fire. Moreover, the hills were bordered by crags and ravines. Since the towers on

the hills stood 18m high and those on level ground 36.5m, they made an astonishing impression on anyone seeing them for the first time – from far away they seemed to be the same height. Inside the city there were further fortifications defending the royal palace, together with the fortress of the Antonia with its awesome turrets… The Temple was designed like a citadel, enclosed by walls that were thicker and more elaborate than anywhere else.

The city incorporated two spurs of land, between which ran the Tyropoeon Valley. The Temple Mount stood on the eastern spur, linked to the Antonia fortress at its north-western corner, with the Ophel Hill immediately to its south. The western spur was much longer, wider and higher, and terminated at Mount Zion. It was in this area the elite Upper City had developed during the Hasmonean and Herodian periods; at its north-western edge stood Herod's Palace. By comparison, the Lower City was much older and accommodated the rest of the city's population. On three sides of the city there were deep ravines, the Hinnom Valley to the west and south and the Kidron Valley to the east between the Ophel Hill and Mount of Olives. The entire Upper and Lower City was enclosed by the First Wall, but as the city had continued its expansion northwards the defences had been strengthened by two further walls.

The Second Wall ran from the Antonia in the east to the Gennath Gate in the west. The Third Wall enclosed a larger area to the north where a suburb known as the New City was under development on the Bezetha Hill. Herod Agrippa had commissioned the building of the wall in AD 41–44 and massive stone blocks had been used in its construction, but because the Romans had become suspicious, Agrippa, as client king and ally of Rome, was forced to abandon the project, hence the ease by which Cestius Gallus was able to seize the New City back in AD 66. Over the intervening four years the rebels had put the final touches to it and completed the wall. They raised its height to 9m at the level of the battlemented walkway, placing on it a series of square towers that projected from the wall at various intervals thereby giving a higher elevation. In addition to the fortifications and difficult ground, the built up part of the city was a maze of narrow streets and alleys, and underground there were a series of water and sewer tunnels, which meant that sorties could emerge from any direction and take the Romans completely by surprise.

Hunkering down to take advantage of these formidable defences, the garrison of Jerusalem at a conservative estimate amounted to over 20,000 well-armed troops, who still possessed the artillery they had captured from the Romans at Beth Horon.

Many of the fighters were refugees, in the words of Tacitus, 'the most indomitable spirits'

Interior view from the Citadel. The Hippicus Tower was named after a friend of Herod who fell in battle, while the Miriamne Tower was named after Herod's wife. (Author's Collection)

because they had no homes or families left they could return to. Among them were 2,000 Tiberians, burning for revenge. Simon b. Gioras had 10,000 followers under 50 officers, and he had been joined by 5,000 Idumeans led by eight commanders, of whom the senior were Jacob b. Sosias and Simon b. Cathlas. John of Gischala had about 6,000 men and 20 officers, supplemented by the 2,400 Zealots under the subordinated Eleazar b. Simon.

Simon occupied the Upper City, and his men garrisoned the First Wall as far as the Kidron where it curved north from the pool at Siloam and went downward to the palaces of the kings of Adiabene. John held the Temple and much of the surrounding neighbourhood, including Ophel and the Tyropoeon Valley. The two leaders had already wrecked the area in between, demolishing houses to get a clearer field of fire at each other.

The political infighting was hardly conducive to effective management of the war effort. But the true Achilles Heel of the defence was the civilian population crammed within the walls. Tacitus and Josephus give us extraordinary figures, but whatever the total, this number had been swollen far in excess of its normal extent by the hordes of pilgrims who had entered Jerusalem to observe Passover and found themselves trapped when Titus arrived.

The pool at Siloam, supplemented by huge cisterns that trapped the rain, adequately met the city's need for fresh water. The problem was food. Much of the grain stored in and around the Temple complex had gone up in smoke as the rival factions battled for control of the streets. The pinch of hunger would soon grip the populace, driving many into increasingly daring – or desperate – forays into the surrounding countryside in search of sustenance.

Titus gave orders to build and fortify a joint camp for *legiones XII* and *XV* at a spot about a kilometre from the walls, with another camp 550m further back for *legio V Macedonica*. Realizing his men must be exhausted after a night march, he wanted them to be out of range of the enemy so that they could get some rest before they began to dig entrenchments. They had scarcely started work when *legio V Macedonica* arrived and was ordered to camp a kilometre away east of the city on the Mount of Olives.

Josephus notes it was only now, with the enemy at the gates, that 'the mutual dissension of the factions within the town, hitherto incessantly at strife, was checked by the war from without'. Upon arriving at the city Titus had impetuously gone forward with an inadequate escort to personally survey the defences and nearly been snared by a sudden Jewish assault. Now, seeing the Roman army dispersed and labouring to set up camps, the two rival factions united their forces for a sortie in force, boiling out of the eastern and southern gateways of the city and charging across the Kidron against *legio X Fretensis* on the Mount of Olives.

Caught off guard the legionaries were cut down in droves. Encouraged by the sortie's success, reinforcements rushed out from the city and in a short space of time threw the Romans out of their uncompleted camp. Titus arrived with his bodyguard and counterattacked the Jews from the flank, driving them back down into the ravine. Assuming the enemy had been sufficiently cowed, Titus ordered *legio X Fretensis* back to work on their camp. But instead of retreating into the city, the Jews received reinforcements and launched a second assault up the slopes of the Mount of Olives, 'hurling themselves [at the Romans] like ferocious wild beasts', according to Josephus.

The Romans broke and ran for the heights, leaving Titus and a handful of men isolated on the lower slopes and hemmed in by the enemy. After finally regrouping, the legionaries countercharged downhill, pushing the Jews once more into the ravine. Titus again gave orders for *legio X Fretensis* to complete their camp, and this was finally accomplished. However, the Jews had sent a clear signal they were not resigned to passively waiting for

TITUS CUTS HIS WAY FREE OF AN AMBUSH UNDER THE WALLS OF JERUSALEM (PP. 56–57)

With the surrounding country effectively pacified, in the spring of AD 70 Titus, the son of the Emperor Vespasian charged with bringing Judea finally to heel, concentrated his forces against Jerusalem. On the morning of 23 April he rode down from Mount Scopus at the head of 600 cavalry, following the road that led towards the main gate through the city's Third Wall, its outermost, covering the approaches to the Bezetha, the New City north of the Temple district (1).

While riding past ancient Jewish royal tomb monuments some distance short of the gate, he swung off the road to the right, aiming for the Psephinus Tower, the tall octagonal structure dominating the north-west corner of the Third Wall. His intent seems to have been to undertake a personal reconnaissance so as to get a better feel for the nature of the defences he would shortly be matched against.

Titus had either been beguiled into a false sense of security owed to the ease by which he had been able to approach the city, or was too brashly arrogant to notice he was entering the ideal terrain in which to set a trap. The land around the city was in many places steeply sloping and uneven, and in others it was terraced and divided into gardens, orchards and olive groves by networks of ditches, hedges, fences, walls, paths and steps. There was a clutter of upstanding rocks, water-troughs, olive presses and stone structures, torn down to afford the defenders a clear field of fire and deny the besiegers any cover (2).

Only part of the Roman force had followed Titus off the road when, without warning, a strong Jewish force sortied out from the so-called 'Women's Towers' (3) through the gate facing the monuments of Queen Helena of Adiabene (4) and cut the column in two. The men still on the road fled, leaving Titus and his escort encircled and in danger of being pinned against the city walls.

The Jewish fighters are armed with a hodge-podge of weapons and armour, much of it looted from the Romans (5). The rest is locally manufactured or derived from Parthian, Arab or other sources.

Despite having haughtily neglected to wear either helmet or breastplate, Titus had no choice but to draw his own sword and personally lead the charge to hack his own way out of the ambush (6). According to Josephus, he 'diverted those perpetually with his sword that came on his side, and overturned many of those that directly met him, and made his horse ride over those that were overthrown' (7). Following their young Caesar's lead, most of his escort also broke through, though many were wounded. Two were not so lucky; one was cut down by Jewish missiles (8), the other surrounded, dragged from his horse, and hacked to death (9).

The Rampart walk on the East Wall north of the Temple Mount, the Dome of Rock in the background. The fact the ground slopes steeply down into the Kidron Valley at this location made siege operations impracticable. (Bibleplaces.com)

Rome to set the terms of the siege. They would aggressively exploit any opportunity to lash out at the besiegers. Titus had underestimated the garrison – given he had personally been caught off guard and surrounded on two consecutive days, nearly fatally so.

Chastened, after posting strong bodies of horse and foot to ward off further sorties, Titus ordered the ground between the Roman camps and the city levelled by felling trees, throwing down hedges and fences, filling in ditches and demolishing projecting rocks. The intent was twofold. First, to deny the guerrilla fighters a friendly environment outside the city; on the open slope they would be exposed to Roman counterattacks. Second, clearing the approaches to the city walls would facilitate the advance of the siege engines and assault parties.

Stymied by the ravines, Titus elected to focus his attack on the western flank of the Third Wall, between the Psephinus Tower and the Western Gate. His plan was to smash through the first two walls, and then through the Old Wall, so that he would be able to push on into the Upper City and capture the Antonia, and finally the Temple. He redeployed his army accordingly. Leaving *legio* X *Fretensis* in their camp on the Mount of Olives, he shifted the others to two new camps about 400m west of the city, V *Macedonica* opposite the Western Gate, *legiones* XII and XV opposite the Psephinus Tower.

The three legions now facing the western flank of the Third Wall were each ordered to construct an earth-and-timber ramp. Repeated Jewish sorties by day and night slowed progress but, covered by the suppressing fire of their artillery, the Roman advance was inexorable. When the ramps were completed Titus ordered forward three battering rams.

The East Wall of the Old City of Jerusalem; in the distance the Golden Gate can be made out. This was usually a quiet sector for the defence unless they were taking the initiative by launching a sortie across the Kidron Valley and up the Mount of Olives. (Bibleplaces.com)

The thudding of the rams against the walls echoed throughout the city, a sound so ominous it induced Simon and John's militias to cease their own personal feud and combine against the common enemy. Josephus describes how in repeated sorties, 'the bolder spirits sprang forward in tight groups' to attack the rams by climbing onto the roofs, tearing off the hurdles, and pelting the crews below with missiles. As they did so, incendiaries were hurled down from the battlements to set the engines alight, and a hail of other missiles was directed at the archers and cavalry stationed around them. At one point, catching the Romans off guard by emerging from a postern door in the wall next to the Hippicus Tower, a large detachment of Jews got in among the rams with firebrands and could have done serious damage had Titus not led a counterattack with his cavalry, driving them back into the city.

Roman engineers had now completed three siege towers, virtually invulnerable to sorties as they were too heavy to overturn and, being encased in an iron carapace, fully fireproof. Titus moved them forward to the city wall. One had been badly constructed and collapsed during the night, the awful clamour briefly spreading panic among the Romans. The surviving pair of *helepoles* ('city-takers') enabled close-in fire support for the ram crews by raining arrows, javelins and sling stones down on the ramparts to keep them clear of defenders.

Agrippa's Wall began to crumble under ceaseless blows from the biggest ram, wryly dubbed *Nikon* ('Victor') by the Jews out of respect for its remorseless progress. By now, the defenders in this sector were exhausted and demoralized by the loss of the Idumean Jacob b. Sosias, who had been cut down by an archer. When the Romans finally punched a breach through the wall on the 15th day of the siege, the decision was taken not to contest the issue further. The defenders withdrew to the Second Wall. Titus occupied the New City and built a new camp in its north-western corner, an area traditionally known as the Camp of the Assyrians because the army of Sennacherib had encamped there in 721 BC.

Unwilling to lose any momentum, the Romans immediately moved their rams up to the Second Wall. John now finally recognized Simon's supreme command of the city's defence, but there was still no integration of the fighters as the two men split the sectors they were responsible for. John's militias took up station on the eastern end of the line, anchored by the Antonia, while Simon's men were concentrated to the west.

The focus of the Roman attack was the central Tower Gate where the two factions met. After just four days one of the rams brought it down. The breach was apparently undefended, and the Romans advanced into the Second City, a warren of narrow streets, courtyards and ramshackle buildings, usually echoing with the commerce of small businesses, but now eerily silent.

Though it seemed deserted, the defenders had merely gone to ground. Without warning the trap was sprung. Under constant missile and hit-and-run attack, the legionaries formed tight blocks behind shield-walls and fought their way back to the breach. It was no more than a narrow gap at the top of a heap of rubble; only a handful of the fleeing Romans could get through at a time, and they risked being struck down by enemy missiles as they did so.

Only the arrival of contingents of archers to give covering fire enabled the bulk of the legionaries to escape. The Jews then surged back onto the Second Wall, barricaded the breach, and held it for another three days. During this struggle, 'assaults, wall-fighting, sorties at unit strength went on continuously all day long', Josephus recalled; 'dusk hardly availed to break off the battles begun at dawn, and there was no sleep for either side ... both passed the night in arms'.

Interior of the Burnt House. This dwelling, which was excavated in the Upper City, may have been the abode of the Kathros family, one of those mentioned in the Talmud as abusing their authority as priests of the Temple. It was destroyed by the fires that raged through Jerusalem in AD 70. (Bibleplaces.com)

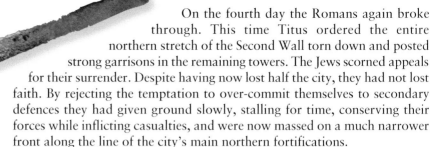

This spearhead, presumably belonging to a rebel fighter, was discovered leaning against the corner of a room in the Burnt House. (Bibleplaces.com)

On the fourth day the Romans again broke through. This time Titus ordered the entire northern stretch of the Second Wall torn down and posted strong garrisons in the remaining towers. The Jews scorned appeals for their surrender. Despite having now lost half the city, they had not lost faith. By rejecting the temptation to over-commit themselves to secondary defences they had given ground slowly, stalling for time, conserving their forces while inflicting casualties, and were now massed on a much narrower front along the line of the city's main northern fortifications.

John's Galileans and Zealots held the Temple Mount and the Antonia Fortress at the eastern end of this line, while Simon's Judeans and Idumeans held the First Wall along its course westwards to the Royal Palace. This defensive line stretched for a distance of about 1,200m, and the Jews had 20 men for every metre of this front. The final struggle for Jerusalem was about to begin.

Titus now split his four legions into two army groups and ordered the construction of four more siege ramps. *Legiones X* and *XV* raised their ramps against the angle of the First and Second walls opposite the Pool of the Patriarch's Bath and the Tomb of John Hyrcanus. Further east, *legiones V* and *XII* raised their ramps over the Struthion Pool against the Antonia. These dispositions indicate that Titus intended to make two simultaneous assaults against the Antonia and the western corner of the First Wall. If both assaults succeeded, he would be able to storm the Temple on two sides, from the Antonia on its northern flank and from the Upper City to the west.

The legionaries worked round the clock on the paired ramps, which were completed on 29 May after 17 days of exhausting toil. The Antonia was the key to the Temple Mount, but it was no soft target. According to Josephus, the ramparts were 18m tall, with turrets at all four corners, three of them 23m high, and one 32m. On the eastern, northern and western sides were deep, wide, rock-cut ravines, which endowed the fortress with even greater effective elevation. On the southern side it was connected to the Temple colonnades by access stairways.

Bridging the ravines fronting the Antonia was carried out under incessant attack from missiles and sorties, the rebels' armoury including some 300 bolt-shooters and 40 stone-throwers, equipment seized from Cestius Gallus four years earlier, in the use of which they were increasingly proficient. Titus immediately gave orders for the troops to bring up the battering rams and the siege towers in preparation for an all-out assault on the Old Wall.

Again, Titus was in for a surprise. The Jews had been taught how to mine by a contingent of Jewish soldiers from Adiabene who were skilled sappers. John's men tunnelled beneath the ground between the Old Wall and the siege lines, undermining the ramps to such an extent that – unknown to the Romans – they were resting only on pit props. The Jews filled the space with faggots covered in pitch and bitumen and then set everything alight.

Without warning, the two ramps in the Antonia area collapsed with a deafening roar into the chasms that opened up below, taking the siege towers with them. Dense clouds of smoke billowed from the crater as the fire below was smothered for a moment; then flames erupted as the bitumen reignited and burned steadily. The Romans were dismayed at the sudden, dramatic demise of so much of their handiwork and so many of their man-hours. Titus sought to refocus them on their objective by utilizing his surviving ramps to unleash the rams against the First Wall. But the Jews were not done yet.

Two days after John's gambit succeeded, it was Simon's turn. Three 'natural fighters' under his command charged out to attack the rams already in operation against the wall. Josephus identifies them as a Galilean called Tephthaeus, a former bodyguard of Agrippa II's sister Mariamne named Megassarus, and a half-crippled volunteer from Adiabene nicknamed Ceagiras. 'In the whole course of the war, the city produced no one more heroic than these three, or more terrifying,' Josephus comments; 'they neither hesitated nor shrank back, but charged through the centre of the foe and set the engines on fire. Pelted with missiles and thrust at with swords on every side, they refused to withdraw from their perilous position until the engines were ablaze.'

Rushing out from their camps when they saw the flames roaring skywards in the dark, the legionaries tried desperately to save the rams, attempting to drag them out of the fire since the hurdles covering them were already ablaze. They were prevented by a host of Jews, who poured out from the postern gates in the First Wall and precipitated a pitched battle, pulling the rams back by their iron carapace, although by now it was red-hot. When the rams finally caught fire, followed by the platforms, the demoralized legionaries gave up in despair.

The Jews, more of whom now swarmed out from the city to join in the fighting, became so encouraged that they pursued the Romans back through the rubble of the northern suburbs to their camp, setting fire to the stockades and attacking the astonished sentries. Only the arrival of Titus, who galloped over from the Antonia, where he had been choosing sites for the new ramps, stabilized the situation. His cavalry charged the Jewish flank; the Jews held their ground stubbornly but finally retreated, step by step, back to the First Wall.

It was the high water mark of the defensive campaign. At that moment, the entire outcome of the siege was hanging in the balance. Gazing on the smouldering ruins of weeks of backbreaking labour the following morning, the Roman rank and file were, if not demoralized, certainly discouraged. It was approaching midsummer, the hottest season of the year. Water, which had to be brought up by mule convoys from distant sources, was in short supply. And the defiance of the enemy was only becoming more brazen as their defences became more formidable.

To both improve security and restore his men's flagging morale Titus ordered the construction of a wall of circumvallation that would completely cut Jerusalem off from the outside world. Welcoming this opportunity to display their resolve – while keeping a safe distance from the city, for now – the legions set to work with a will.

When completed, the wall ran from Roman headquarters east through the New City and the Kidron to the Mount of Olives. Then it bent to the south of Siloam before turning west and then north again around Herod's mausoleum until it returned to the Camp of the Assyrians. Nearly 8km long, 13 forts strengthened the wall, each of which was 60m in circumference. Thanks to the legionaries' unflagging enthusiasm, the whole structure was finished in three days, a 'well-nigh incredible' feat, as Josephus says.

The shroud of famine now descended in earnest over the city. Previously, enterprising civilians had dared risk nocturnal excursions into the surrounding countryside in search of food. Now there was no hope of succour, and Titus twisted the knife relentlessly, ordering all those rebels snared outside the walls crucified in full view of the ramparts.

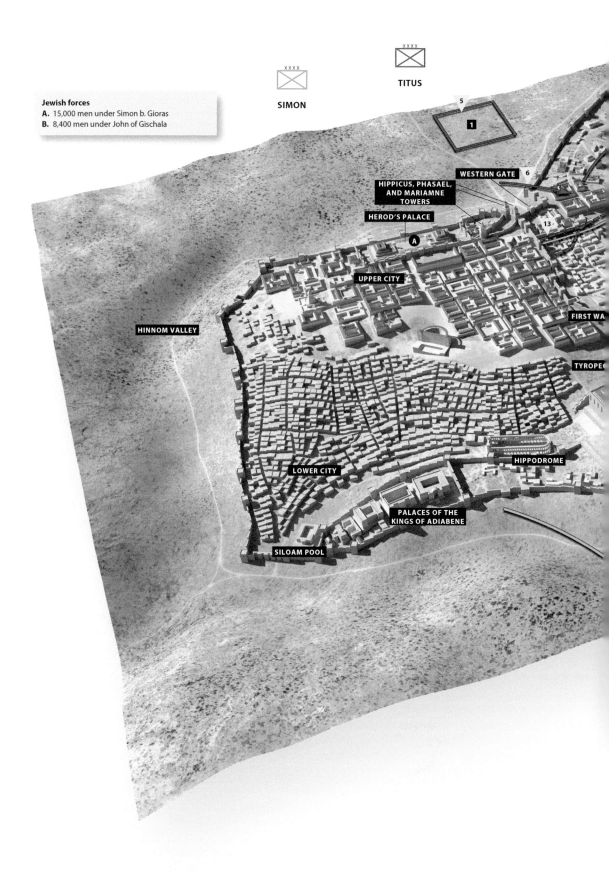

SIMON

xxxx

TITUS

xxxx

Jewish forces
A. 15,000 men under Simon b. Gioras
B. 8,400 men under John of Gischala

5

1

WESTERN GATE 6

HIPPICUS, PHASAEL, AND MARIAMNE TOWERS

HEROD'S PALACE

13

A

UPPER CITY

FIRST WA

HINNOM VALLEY

TYROPE

HIPPODROME

LOWER CITY

PALACES OF THE KINGS OF ADIABENE

SILOAM POOL

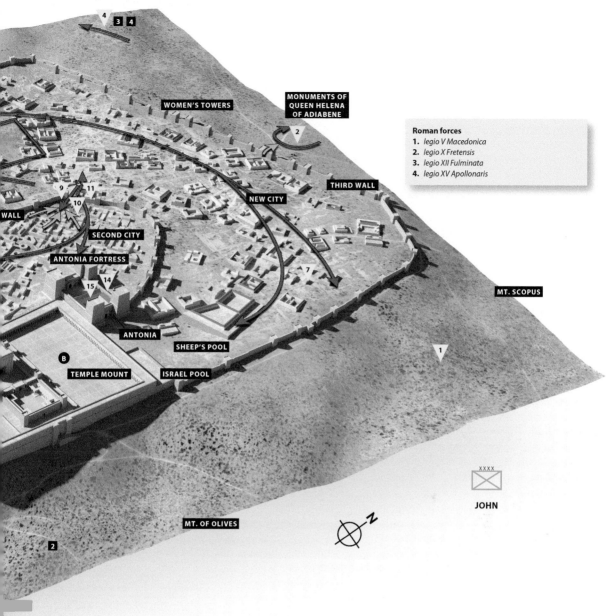

Roman forces
1. *legio V Macedonica*
2. *legio X Fretensis*
3. *legio XII Fulminata*
4. *legio XV Apollonaris*

WOMEN'S TOWERS

MONUMENTS OF
QUEEN HELENA
OF ADIABENE

THIRD WALL

NEW CITY

WALL

SECOND CITY

ANTONIA FORTRESS

MT. SCOPUS

ANTONIA

SHEEP'S POOL

TEMPLE MOUNT

ISRAEL POOL

JOHN

MT. OF OLIVES

EVENTS

1. 24 April: Titus encamps *legiones XV, XII* and *V* on Mt Scopus to the north-east of the city.

2. Titus is ambushed and nearly caught while leading a scouting party too close to the Third Wall.

3. Titus orders *legio X Fretensis* to encamp on the Mount of Olives east of the city. A major Jewish sortie across the Kidron Valley catches the Romans off guard while they are engaged in construction; Titus personally leads reinforcements to drive the Jews back into the city.

4. Titus redeploys *legiones XII* and *XV* to a camp opposite the Psephinus Tower.

5. Titus redeploys *legio V Macedonica* to a camp opposite the Western Gate.

6. *Legiones XII, XV* and *V* construct three siege ramps. Covered by suppressing fire from their siege towers, and shrugging of Jewish sorties, Roman battering rams punch a breach in the Third Wall.

7. As the Jews retire to the Second Wall the Romans occupy, and raze, the New City.

8. Titus advances to a new camp located in the Camp of the Assyrians.

9. Roman rams bring down the tower at the junction of the Second Wall. The Romans enter the Second City.

10. Jewish forces infiltrate Roman lines, drive the legionaries back through the breach, and reoccupy the Second Wall.

11. The Romans again breach the Second Wall.

12. As the Jews retire to the Third Wall the Romans occupy the Second City.

13. *Legiones X* and *XV* construct ramps against the First Wall.

14. *Legiones V* and *XII* construct ramps against the Antonia.

15. Jewish defenders undermine the ramps raised against the Antonia.

16. Jewish sortie destroys the ramps raised against the First Wall.

17. The Jews drive the Romans back to their camp.

18. Titus leads a counterattack that hits the Jews in their flank; the Jews retreat back to the First Wall.

THE SIEGE OF JERUSALEM, AD 70
Titus' legions invest the city and take the outer suburbs.

Model of the Antonia Fortress, from the Israel Museum, Jerusalem. Possession of the Antonia (named by Herod the Great in honour of his friend, the triumvir Mark Antony) was the key to the Temple Mount. (Deror Avi via Wikipedia)

Within the city the situation grew worse with each passing day. Streets once bustling with life lay empty and silent as the war-weary population subsided into apathy. 'Amidst all this misery there was little weeping or wailing,' Josephus recorded. 'Starvation had killed all sense of affection, so that the slowly dying gazed with dry eyes and open mouths at anyone who had passed away before them.'

With the dwindling reserves of food reserved for the fighters, non-combatants were reduced to boiling straw and drinking the juice. In one incident, hunger drove a woman to such an extreme of madness she murdered, roasted and ate her own child. But even with the city slowly dying around them, like clockwork the priests upheld the holy rite of Tamid, the daily sacrifice at the Temple of a lamb to Yahweh. Secular politics was one thing; wars, empires and dynasties might come and go; but to the pious, it was the commitment to upholding their ancient religious law that defined the Jewish nation.

However, more and more of the less devout were prepared to surrender and opt for a life of slavery in preference to a slow death from hunger. Many were cheated of even this faint succour; thousands were eviscerated upon reaching Roman lines by auxiliaries eager to seize the gold Jews were believed to swallow in order to smuggle it out of the city.

The Zealot response to this steady trickle of defections was a policy of savage reprisal. Several eminent – and wealthy – members of the priestly families were made an example of. One of them was Matthias b. Boethus. He and those three of his four sons the Zealots had been able to round up were sentenced to death on charges of collaboration. Reminding Simon that it was he who had invited him into Jerusalem, Matthias begged to be executed before his sons. His request was denied. After witnessing his sons being slaughtered before his eyes, Matthias was led to the wall to see, Simon remarked, whether his Roman friends would assist him. Then he was killed. Nor would Simon allow any of them burial.

Titus now concentrated his entire force against the Antonia. The nearby hills having been stripped bare, he sent his men deep into the hinterland to cut timber, leaving 'nothing but desert and stumps of trees,' according to Josephus. It took the Romans three weeks to complete the construction of four massive platforms against the Antonia. 'The completion of the earthworks proved, to the Romans no less than the Jews, a source of apprehension,' Josephus notes. 'For while the latter thought that, should they fail to burn these also, the city would be taken, the Romans feared that they would never take it, should these embankments too be destroyed. For there was a dearth of materials and the soldiers bodies were stinking beneath their toils and their minds under a succession of reverses.'

But Roman resolve held and, as the siege entered its tenth week, they commenced a full-scale assault, deploying both battering rams against the Antonia and men equipped with crowbars to lever out stones at its base.

When the Romans withdrew at the end of the first day they apparently had very little to show for their efforts. However, they had in fact made a great deal more progress than they supposed. The tunnel John's sappers had dug in May passed directly beneath the Antonia. Under pressure from the great weight of masonry, timber, earth, machines and men pressing against it, weakened by the relentless pounding of the rams, and with the ground softened by a heavy rain, the foundations suddenly collapsed during the night – and into the void tumbled the northern wall of the Antonia.

The event was a shock to both sides, but the Romans were in for another. Eager to follow up on this unanticipated gift from the gods, at first light they found that behind the rubble John's men had already constructed a second wall in anticipation the first would fall. Determined to sustain the momentum, Titus sought volunteers for a frontal assault on the Jewish positions. Unsurprisingly, only a dozen men responded, for 'manifestly destruction awaited its first assailants'. Led by a wiry, dark-skinned Syrian auxiliary called Sabinus, this handful of men launched an assault so audacious it seems to have caught the defenders by surprise. Though missiles cut several down during their approach, the remnant, led by Sabinus, succeeded in climbing the wall and scattering the defenders. They were far too few, however, and there was no second wave coming up in support behind them. Sabinus tripped, fell and died under a barrage of missiles as he tried to raise himself up behind his shield. Three others were battered to death with stones on top of the wall. The eight who were wounded in front of the wall were carried away by their comrades. The attack had been foolhardy and irresponsible, and it left the men who had watched it with no stomach for another daylight assault.

The cover of darkness, however, was a great equalizer. Two days later, in the early hours of 5 July, on their own initiative 20 legionaries on duty guarding the platforms, accompanied by a standard-bearer of *legio V Macedonica*, a trumpeter and two cavalry troopers, crept silently forwards and climbed into the ruins of the Antonia. They slit the throats of the sleeping Jewish sentries, and, after scaling the wall, ordered the trumpeter to sound a signal. The other sentries on duty fled, 'before any had noted what number had ascended, for the panic and the trumpet call led them to imagine that the enemy had mounted in force'.

Titus and other senior officers led a contingent of picked men into the ruins to consolidate this almost anticlimactic success. Total victory seemed within his grasp, for in the darkness and confusion most of the Jews had fled right back across the Sanctuary concourse to the Temple. The leading Roman elements now tried to follow them by pouring down the passages constructed by Herod the Great to link the fortress to the Temple.

Those passages were the last chokepoint available to the Jews if they had any hope of maintaining a defensive perimeter. If the Romans succeeded in flooding onto the wide-open space of the Sanctuary they would be in a position to turn the flank of the Jewish garrisons on the northern and western colonnades and isolate the rebels who had taken refuge in the Temple. But the fighters from both John's and Simon's militias now combined to block the Roman advance, and a desperate struggle erupted in the narrow spaces

The retaining wall on its western flank is all that remains above ground of Herod's Temple Mount. The massive stone blocks are mute testament to its grandeur – and the challenge it presented to the Roman besiegers. (Author's Collection)

at the tunnel entrances. Both sides were aware of the stakes: 'Those in front must either kill or be killed – there could be no retreat – for on either side those behind pressed their own men forwards and left no space between the opposing lines,' Josephus comments.

The Romans excelled at close-quarters combat, but because their advance was channelled down the narrow confines of the passages they were unable to mass and form for a charge. The Jews, on the other hand, with huge reserves of men backed up across the concourse behind them, were able to keep the Romans penned in at the entrances and to provide a constant stream of reinforcements to their own front line.

'At length, Jewish fury prevailing over Roman skill,' Josephus records; 'the whole line began to waver. For they had been fighting from the ninth hour of the night until the seventh of the day … the Romans with but a portion of their forces, the legions upon whom the present combatants were dependent having not yet come up. It was therefore considered sufficient for the present to hold the Antonia.' At one in the afternoon – 11 hours after the stealth attack on the Antonia – their officers pulled the legions back.

The legions had been repulsed, but they were still poised like a dagger at the exposed heart of the Jewish state. In order to attack the Temple on as broad a front as possible, Titus ordered the Antonia razed to the ground. This took his troops a week to accomplish. On 17 July, eager to land the decisive blow, Titus, hoping to catch the Jews off guard, ordered a night assault on the Temple complex. Still unable to deploy his full strength in the space available, and prevented from covering the attack adequately with artillery, archers and slingers because the Jews still held the northern and western colonnades, he pulled the 30 best men from each century in the line and marshalled them in 1,000-strong cohorts commanded by tribunes.

The attack was to be led by Sextus Cerialis, legate of *legio V Macedonica*, while Titus and other senior officers occupied an elevated observation post in one of the surviving Antonia towers. An hour before dawn, having moved as silently as possible into line in the hope of catching the Jewish sentries unawares, perhaps as many as 7,200 legionaries advanced to the attack. The sentries were alert, however; the alarm was immediately raised, and thousands of militiamen were soon rushing to find places in an improvised line. The leading Roman ranks came to a halt and the column concertinaed as the rear ranks stumbled in the darkness against those ahead.

In places, disoriented and panicked Romans cut down fellow legionaries. The same happened on the Jewish side, where the line was a shambles, its attacks and retreats badly controlled, the men frequently colliding into each other unexpectedly in the gloom.

It was only when the sun came up that the ragged lines on both sides could be shaken out and given order. The space was so cramped there was no room for manoeuvre. The ensuing fight resembled a battle on a stage, thought Josephus, and in fact more closely resembled a pitched battle between heavy infantry than any other encounter in the war: 'The two sides separated into opposing formations and began to hurl missiles in an orderly engagement. Neither side gave an inch or showed any sign of weariness. In the main the battle was stationary, the ebb and flow very slight and sudden. Flight and pursuit were alike impossible.' Titus spent the morning barking orders from the heights of the Antonia, but to little avail. After battling from before dawn to nearly midday both sides disengaged, 'without either side having really budged the other from the spot where the first blow was struck, and without any decision being reached'.

Unable to force his way through the Jewish lines, Titus would have to bring them down, stone by stone. He ordered the construction of another four siege platforms against the north-western corner of the Temple Mount. Once more the legions set to work, forced to labour at high summer in full armour, for Jewish missile fire and sorties were relentless, and there was continual skirmishing between the front lines on the Temple Mount, the Romans massed near the ruins of the Antonia, the Jews on the northern side of the Inner Court of the Temple.

Elsewhere, the defence remained surprisingly active. There was a raid to seize horses that Roman cavalrymen out looking for firewood or fodder were in the habit of leaving to graze freely near the walls, and a large-scale attack on the Roman outposts on the Mount of Olives, perhaps an unsuccessful attempt to break through the wall of circumvallation and ease the blockade.

Aware that another – and this time full-scale – assault might come at any moment, the Zealots burned down the north-western colonnade that joined the Temple to the Antonia. Two days later, when the Romans set the adjoining colonnade on fire, the defenders pulled down the roof so as to destroy any remaining communication with the Antonia.

A few days after this, on 27 July, the Jews set a successful trap for the Romans working on one of the platforms being built against the western colonnade. Though the northern extent of this colonnade had now been destroyed, the Roman platform was being raised against the surviving section near the broken end. At this point the Jews secretly filled the spaces between the rafters and the ceiling below with a flammable mixture of dry wood, bitumen and pitch. They then made a show of withdrawing from this part of the colonnade.

Many of the Romans working on the platform below sensed an opportunity and ran forwards with ladders to mount an immediate assault by escalade. Hundreds quickly reached the top of the undefended wall and climbed out onto the roof of the colonnade. At that point the Jews ignited their firetrap and engulfed their enemies in flames.

The boost in morale the Jews enjoyed from this success was swiftly undermined by the gravest of ill omens. It was on the 17th day of the month of Tammuz in the Hebrew calendar, about 5 August, when reality proved it could no longer be denied by even the most stubborn levels of devotion. The priests were forced to suspend the holy rite of Tamid, the daily sacrifice of a lamb, as the supply of fresh victims had finally run out. The significance for the defenders can only be imagined.

THE SIEGE OF THE TEMPLE MOUNT APPROACHES ITS CLIMAX (PP. 70–71)

Three months after the siege commenced, even though the Romans had penetrated the Third and Second Walls and seized the Antonia Fortress that dominated the northern approach to the Temple complex itself, the Jewish defenders of Jerusalem, alone, surrounded, and starving, were still full of fight. Towards the end of July they successfully lured the Romans into a trap.

By this point the Romans had secured a foothold on the northern end of the Temple Mount and were forcing the defenders to disperse their manpower by raising a series of siege platforms against its flanks.

The outer court of the Temple Mount was surrounded by a colonnade 30 cubits wide, constituting a portico comprised of three rows of columns 25 cubits high and made of a single piece of white marble. The interior ceiling of the portico was lined with cedar. Though the northern extent of the western colonnade, where it connected to the Antonia, had now been destroyed, a Roman platform was being raised against the surviving section near its broken end **(1)**.

On 27 July Jews gave the impression of falling back from this section of the colonnade. In fact, they had quietly filled the spaces between the rafters and the ceiling with highly flammable timber, bitumen and pitch.

Seeing the Jews withdraw, and sensing what they assumed was a golden opportunity to outflank the Jewish defences on the Temple Mount, the Romans working on the siege platform raised scaling ladders and rushed to the top to seize the colonnade. With hundreds of the enemy now in possession of the roof, the Jews sprung their trap, igniting the flammable material packed underneath it **(2)**.

Surrounded in moments by roaring flames and wreaths of choking smoke, their ladders immolated, and the colonnade collapsing beneath them **(3)**, the Romans isolated there are out of options. Some hurl themselves down into the city **(4)**, others behind enemy lines into the Temple Mount **(5)**, where their broken bones leave them easy prey for Jewish fighters **(6)**. 'Most', according to Josephus, 'for all their haste, were too slow for the fire, though a few cheated the flames with their own daggers' **(7)**. Those who try to fight their way out by pushing south along the colonnade run up against the Jewish defenders there **(8)**. With their best fighters in the front ranks, many of them accoutred in stolen Roman arms and armour, the Jews allow none of the Romans desperately flinging themselves at their shield wall to escape.

Unaware of this spiritual crisis, Titus ordered a fresh assault on the Temple Mount. Day after day his men worked round the clock, presumably in shifts, protected overhead by hurdles and locked shields against the continuous bombardment of boulders, firebrands and other missiles that rained down from above. The rams seemed to make no impact on the wall, however; the huge size of the blocks, the close-bonded construction, and the thickness of the masonry defied the best Rome could throw at them. With tremendous effort the working parties attempting to lever blocks from the base of the walls with crowbars had succeeded in prizing free four stones, but there was such depth to the edifice that this had no effect on the stability of the structure.

Frustrated once more, Titus abandoned the attempt to breach the walls and instead ordered them stormed. The height of the platforms did enable assault by escalade, but his subordinates must have reminded Titus it remained, as always, a strategy unlikely to succeed against a strong garrison and almost certain to result in heavy casualties.

So the assault panned out. Some of the ladders, weighed down by heavy infantry, were pushed from the walls and toppled to the ground. Heavy covering fire from Roman siege artillery sweeping the battlements, however, enabled most of the legionaries to ascend to the parapets; 'The Jews were in no hurry to stop them,' Josephus records, 'but when they climbed up they were violently assailed: some were pushed backwards and sent headlong; others clashed with the defenders and were killed; many, as they stepped off the ladders, were unable to get behind their shields before they were run through with swords.' The Romans even resorted to bringing their eagles up the ladders, in the belief that any legionary would die rather than suffer the indelible disgrace of their loss, but to general astonishment the standards were captured by the defenders, who succeeded in killing everybody who tried to scale the wall in a bid to help them. Disheartened, Titus abandoned the assault.

The Romans then burnt out the remnant of the northern colonnade, right up to the north-eastern corner of the Temple Mount, at the angle overlooking the sharp drop down into the ravine of the Kidron Valley.

The Temple Mount, Herod the Great's reconstruction of the Temple, which doubled the size of the original platform, began in 20 BC and was not fully completed until AD 64, just two years before the revolt broke out. The sudden loss of gainful employment for the city's artisans may have contributed to the general instability in Jerusalem at the time. (Ariely via Wikipedia)

Now that the Temple lay within his grasp, Titus discussed with his subordinates what should be done with this holiest of Jewish structures. Some argued for burning it, for both practical and psychological reasons. Given it was the supreme symbol of Jewish resistance to imperial authority and the focus of a religion that refused to recognize the gods of Rome, while it stood the Jews would never truly be defeated. However, at least in Josephus's account, Titus ruled the Temple be preserved, describing it as 'an ornament to their Empire'.

But in his account, Sulpicius Severus inverts the motivations of the protagonists: 'some thought that a consecrated shrine which was famous beyond all other works of men, ought not to be razed, arguing that its preservation would bear witness to the moderation of Rome, while its destruction would forever brand her cruelty.' However, others, 'including Titus himself,' maintained the destruction of the Temple was a key strategic priority, 'in order to wipe out more completely the religion of the Jews'.

In any event, with the colonnades burnt out, the Jewish position on the outer walls of the Temple Mount was now untenable. Vulnerable to enfilade fire from Roman artillery and archers massed in the ruins of the Antonia, the Jews pulled back to reform their defensive line across the middle of the Sanctuary.

The left of the Jewish line was now anchored on the western gate opposite the Gymnasium, which was linked with the Upper City by a bridge spanning the Tyropoeon Valley and defended by a tower that John had built during his factional struggle with Simon. The right rested on Solomon's Portico, the eastern colonnade of the Sanctuary. The centre of the line ran through the Temple and the Inner Court. The rebels had now been reduced to dependency on the physical security as well as the spiritual inspiration offered by the Temple.

If the Platform Mount was a gigantic fortification, then the Outer Court, part of which the Romans now held, was like an outer bailey, while the Inner Court, still held by the Jews, formed an inner bailey, and the Temple itself a great bastion or keep within this. A chest-high balustrade ran around the outside of the Inner Court, marking the boundary beyond which Gentiles, on pain of death, were not permitted to pass. There were four gateways on both the north and south sides; chambers and colonnades ran around the inside of the wall so there were wide fighting-platforms at rooftop level, which was raised perhaps 20m or more above the surrounding Sanctuary concourse. The eastern half of the interior formed the Court of Women. The western half was elevated above this on a second podium and separated from it by another massive wall.

Beyond the Corinthian Gate, which passed through the middle of this wall, was the narrow Court of the Israelites and beyond this the Court of the Priests. Here, behind the blood-spattered altar, raised up on a third podium, stood the towering edifice of the Temple itself with its white marble façade and enormous golden gates gleaming in the summer sunshine. At the furthest recess of the Temple was the Holy of Holies, the abode of Yahweh himself, where the High Priest alone entered on the Day of Atonement. The flat roof, bristling with golden spikes to keep the birds at bay, rose to the height of 45m.

As the blackened northern rim of the Outer Court gradually filled with legionaries, the Jews, starving and exhausted, fell back from the open spaces of the concourse and took station on the rooftops of the Inner Court and the Temple. A few important deserters continued to drift over to the

The Temple, says Josephus, looked like 'a mountain covered with snow,' so dazzling was its white marble. At 25m high and 21m wide the entrance on the eastern wall was the largest. The father of Tiberius Julius Alexander, who served as second in command under Titus during the siege of Jerusalem, had donated the gold and silver that embossed this, the Beautiful Gate. (Juan D. Cuadra via Wikipedia)

Romans. Among them was Ananus of Ammaus, a notoriously bloodstained member of Simon's bodyguard, and Archelaus b. Maggadatus.

Still the Jews retained sufficient vigour to mount aggressive sorties. At dawn on 9 August they sallied forth in strength from the Eastern Gate. The Romans facing them, though surprised and outnumbered, held their ground behind locked shields, and Titus ordered cavalry counterattacks into the Jewish mass. A confused battle of alternating rushes and retreats continued for three hours. Then, unable to make an impression on the Roman line and threatened with imminent defeat, the Jews withdrew to the Inner Court. Again the following day the Jews attacked the Romans holding the Outer Court. The Roman counterattack pressed the Jews back against the walls of the Temple. Then came the apocalyptic climax to what had evolved from a provincial uprising into a war of cultural annihilation.

Josephus captures the scene: 'At this moment, one of the soldiers, awaiting no orders and with no horror of so dread a deed, but moved by some supernatural impulse, snatched a brand from the burning timber and, hoisted up by one of his comrades, flung the fiery missile through a low golden door which gave access on the north side to the chambers surrounding the Sanctuary.'

With the Court full of highly flammable timbers and textiles, and the whole place bone-dry in the summer heat, fire took hold immediately. The flames and thick black smoke rising from the Temple could be seen everywhere, from the surrounding hills to the city below.

The rebels in the immediate vicinity were trapped on the horns of an impossible dilemma. The holiest place of their religion, containing all its sacred texts and treasures, was also the fortress at the lynchpin of their defensive line. They could not fight the flames and the enemy at the same

The chaos and carnage of the fall of the Temple is vividly captured by Francesco Hayez. According to Josephus, 'on all sides was carnage and flight. Around the altar a pile of corpses was accumulating; down the steps of the Sanctuary flowed a stream of blood, and the bodies of the victims killed above went sliding to the bottom.' (Alfredo Dagli Orti/The Art Archive at Art Resource, NY)

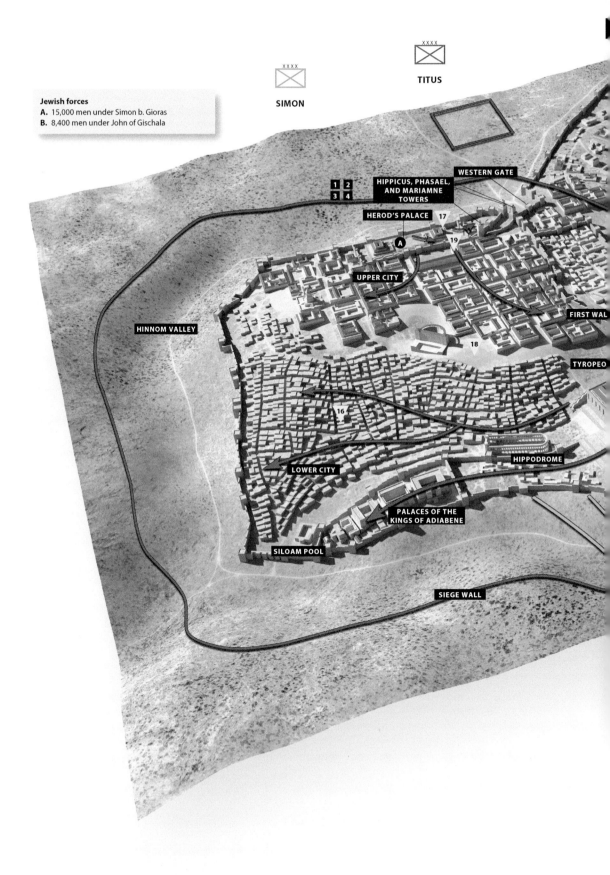

Jewish forces
A. 15,000 men under Simon b. Gioras
B. 8,400 men under John of Gischala

SIMON

TITUS

WESTERN GATE

HIPPICUS, PHASAEL,
AND MARIAMNE
TOWERS

1 2
3 4

HEROD'S PALACE   17

A   19

UPPER CITY

HINNOM VALLEY

FIRST WAL

18

TYROPEO

16

HIPPODROME

LOWER CITY

PALACES OF THE
KINGS OF ADIABENE

SILOAM POOL

SIEGE WALL

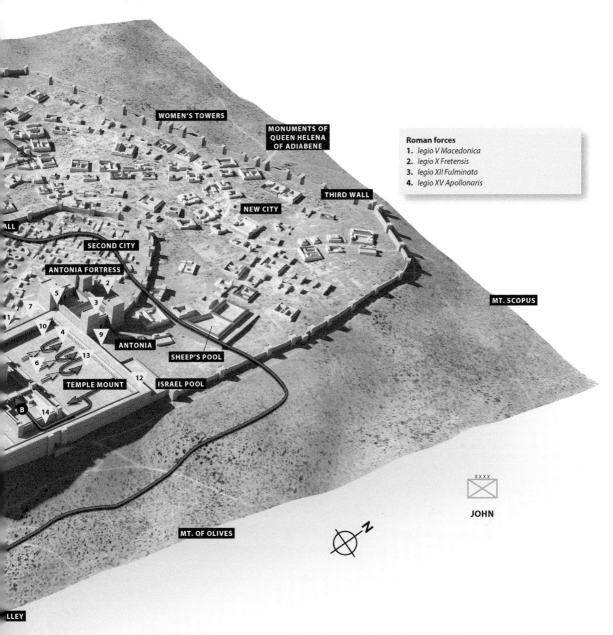

WOMEN'S TOWERS

MONUMENTS OF
QUEEN HELENA
OF ADIABENE

THIRD WALL

Roman forces
1. *legio V Macedonica*
2. *legio X Fretensis*
3. *legio XII Fulminata*
4. *legio XV Apollonaris*

NEW CITY

...ALL

SECOND CITY

ANTONIA FORTRESS

MT. SCOPUS

ANTONIA

SHEEP'S POOL

TEMPLE MOUNT

ISRAEL POOL

MT. OF OLIVES

JOHN

...LLEY

EVENTS

1. Titus orders construction of a wall of circumvallation.

2. The Romans construct four siege ramps against the Antonia.

3. The northern wall of the Antonia collapses.

4. July 5: the Romans seize the Antonia. First battle of the Temple. The Roman bid to break out onto the Temple forecourt is foiled.

5. Titus orders the Antonia destroyed.

6. July 17: second battle of the Temple. The Romans are again repulsed.

7. Titus orders construction of four siege ramps against the north-western corner of the Temple Mount.

8. Ongoing Jewish sorties, including a major attempt on the Mt. of Olives.

9. The Jews destroy the colonnades connecting the Antonia with the Temple Mount.

10. July 27: The Jews set a trap. Rigging the colonnades on the north-western corner of the Temple Mount with a fire trap they feign withdrawal. The Romans advance to occupy the abandoned position and are immolated.

11. Titus orders the Temple Mount stormed. The assault is driven off with heavy losses.

12. The Romans burn out the remaining colonnades on the northern perimeter of the Temple Mount. The Jews pull back to the Temple.

13. August 9: third battle of the Temple.

14. August 10: fourth battle of the Temple. Destruction of the Temple. The Romans seize the entire Temple Mount.

15. August 11: failed parley on the bridge.

16. The Romans burn out the Lower City.

17. August 20: the Romans construct four siege ramps against Herod's Palace.

18. The allies and auxiliaries construct siege ramps against the Upper City.

19. September 7: the Romans assault and take Herod's Palace.

THE FALL OF JERUSALEM, AD 70
The final struggle for the Temple Mount and the Upper and Lower Cities.

time. The legions gave them no respite. The Roman line instinctively surged forwards, apparently without orders, the rank and file eager to seize this serendipitous opportunity to consummate more than three months' toil and sacrifice. Penetrating the Inner Court of the Temple, the building that had hovered just out of their reach for so long, the Romans gave full vent to their rage and frustration. Even while the Temple burnt, Josephus records that 'looting went on right and left, and all who were caught were put to the sword. There was no pity for age, no regard for rank; little children and old men, laymen and priests alike were butchered.' Such was their frenzy, many of the legionaries were trampled to death by their own compatriots. By the time Titus arrived on the scene it was too late to restrain his men, even assuming he had wanted to.

When their lust for murder and plunder was finally sated, the conquerors undertook the ritual tokens that sanctified their victory. While the legionaries chanted 'Imperator! Imperator!' in honour of their leader, Titus ordered an ox, a sheep, and, the most profane, a pig to be sacrificed before the eastern gate of the Temple to consummate the supremacy of the Roman over the Jewish God.

LAST STANDS

The Temple was still smouldering the next morning, but Jewish resistance was not broken yet; Simon's militias remained firmly entrenched in the Upper City and those of John's men who escaped the fall of the Temple had fled to join them there. The many thousands of rebel fighters left still held some strong positions, including Herod's Palace. It was advantageous to both sides to parley, so they met on the viaduct – the bridge that spanned the Tyropoeon Valley between the western gate of the sanctuary and the gymnasium on the eastern slope of the Upper City.

Negotiations did not proceed far. Simon and John wanted free passage out of the dying city; Titus would only offer unconditional surrender and slavery. Titus then unleashed his legions on the Lower City. They burned out the Acra and Ophel districts all the way down to the Pool of Siloam. The council houses, archives and palaces of the kings of Adiabene all went up in flames, as did many houses that were full of dead bodies, filling the air with the stench of burning human flesh.

Clearing the Lower City of rebels took the Romans two days. Reducing the Upper City would be far more problematic as its thickly clustered houses were dominated by the bastions of Herod's Palace. The approach from the east was hindered by the Central Valley, across which Simon had built four fortress-towers during his war with John. In addition, the rebels were making use of the vast network of rock-cut drains and cisterns that ran beneath the city.

It made more sense to assault the palace on its western flank, from the Roman main camp. Since the fortification

Rubble thrown down by Romans during the siege of the Temple still litters the area surrounding the Western Wall. According to the Gospels, Christ foretold the fate of Jerusalem: 'enemies will set up ramparts around you and surround you, and hem you in on every side. They will crush you to the ground, you and your children within you and they will not leave within you one stone upon another.' Luke 19.43–4. (Mark A. Wilson via Wikipedia)

could not be stormed directly, the Romans were left with no choice but to begin, again, the laborious process of building siege platforms.

The four legions were set to work in the Hinnom Valley on 20 August, and over the following two-and-a-half weeks they constructed serviceable platforms against the western wall of the Palace. The allied and auxiliary troops worked on the opposite side of the Upper City, constructing platforms near the Viaduct, the Gymnasium, and Simon's Tower.

By 7 September the Romans were in position to launch their assault. On the face of it, this was a daunting proposition. Herod's Palace was as formidable externally as its interior was sumptuous ('No tongue could describe the magnificence', Josephus rhapsodizes). It was dominated by three towers, the Hippicus, Phasael, and Mariamne, hinging at the angle where the First Wall turned eastwards, their elevation exaggerated because they stood on the crest of a hill. Josephus claims they were superior in size, beauty and strength to any in the world, being constructed from white marble cut in massive blocks so perfectly united that each seemed like a single rock 'sent up by Mother Earth and later cut and polished by artists' hands, into shapes and angles, so invisible from any view point was the filling of the joints'.

The Mariamne tower was 25m high, while the Hippicus tower rose to the height of 36m. Its roof contained a cistern surrounded by a ring of turrets and crowned with ramparts. The Phasael tower soared to 40m; its solid base stands to this day. Simon had made it his headquarters. But a defence is ultimately only as effective as its defenders. The Jewish holdouts were by now only a shadow of the bold fighters who had fought so hard prior to the fall of the Temple. When the rams rumbled forwards some of the rebels abandoned the threatened wall without a fight, and the fire of those who remained was quickly suppressed by the weight of incoming Roman shot.

The crews of the rams were soon working unmolested and sections of the western wall were brought down that very day. The Romans found themselves storming through undefended breaches.

The rebel leaders and their immediate followers had taken refuge in the three northern towers, but even these were abandoned without a fight. With determined men to defend them they were impregnable, but with active resistance disintegrating they were traps. The leaders and other small groups of fighters scattered across the city, seeking ways through the Roman cordon. Most failed and, if not cut down when they ran into parties of soldiers, sought temporary refuge in the gloom of the sewers.

Both John and Simon went underground. John had no agenda beyond staying out of Roman custody and surrendered when his stock of food was exhausted, but Simon actively sought to make his escape. He and a small band sought to dig their way to freedom under the walls, but the distance was too great. When their supplies ran out, Simon, scorning suicide, suddenly materialized amidst the

This milestone erected in Jerusalem by the *legio X Fretensis* salutes Vespasian as Augustus and Titus as Caesar. (Bibleplaces.com)

The great seven-branched menorah looted from the Temple dominates this scene from the Arch of Titus, celebrating his triumph at the conclusion of the war. Note the placards used to inform the spectators about exactly what they were gloating over. The inscription boasts, inaccurately, Titus 'subdued the Jewish people and destroyed the city of Jerusalem, which all generals, kings, and peoples before him had either attacked without success or left entirely unassailed'. (Vanni/Art Resource, NY)

ruins of the Temple, dressed in a short white tunic and crimson cape. We will never know his exact intent. Martyrdom? Bluff? A bid to take advantage of Roman superstition? A final appeal for divine intervention? Whatever his motivation, the Romans were shocked but not panicked by his actions; he was arrested, put in chains and sent to Titus, who by now had returned to Caesarea.

The siege had been the hardest fought and most comprehensive manifestation of Classical Era total war since the fall of Carthage over two centuries earlier. Even by Roman standards, the human toll was appalling. The victors kept 700 of the tallest and best-looking young men for Titus's triumph at Rome. Of the remaining males, those over 17 were sent in chains to a living death as forced labour in Egypt or to arenas all over the Roman Empire where they would die in gladiatorial combats or be fed to wild animals. Women and children were packed off to the slave markets.

Josephus says that only 97,000 prisoners of war had been taken in the entire Judean campaign, while 1,100,000 people had died during the siege of Jerusalem itself. As he is so prone to exaggeration, the estimate of 600,000 dead given by Tacitus seems more plausible, even if still enormous. On the other hand, Josephus justifies his figure by explaining that a large number of the casualties were pilgrims who had been trapped in the city while visiting it for the feast of Passover. In addition, there were all those who had come in from the surrounding countryside in order to take refuge.

The triumph Vespasian staged in Rome to honour his son's Judean victory was the capstone of his efforts to legitimize the Flavian regime (and, hopefully, dynasty). In addition to the 700 captives, the festivities featured floats depicting the most dramatic scenes from the campaign and displays of the Holy treasures plundered from the Temple, including the great seven-branched menorah. The Jewish leaders John and Simon were also paraded through the streets of Rome in the wake of Titus's chariot. Once the exhibition concluded John was, somewhat surprisingly, only subject to life imprisonment.

The Romans had something more dramatic in mind for Simon. When the procession arrived at the temple of Jupiter on the Capitoline he was dragged across the forum and scourged by metal-barbed whips that tore strips of flesh from his body. Then at the place reserved for public executions he was put to death by slow strangulation. The announcement of his demise was hailed by 'shouts of universal applause'. So ended the first Jewish revolt against Rome.

AFTERMATH

BITTER END

Organized resistance in Judea was at an end, but three isolated redoubts – Herodium south of Jerusalem, and Machaerus and Masada, on the eastern and western banks of the Dead Sea respectively – still remained in rebel hands. Vespasian assigned the reduction of these strongholds to Lucilius Bassus, who had served the Flavian cause during the civil war, and for the first 18 months of Vespasian's reign had been equestrian prefect of the fleets at Misenum and Ravenna.

Although occupying strong defensive positions, the garrisons of Herodium and Machaerus had little stomach for a now-futile struggle and swiftly capitulated. The last Jewish refugees from Jerusalem, including a militia commander who had made his way through the city's sewers and slipped unnoticed through the Roman lines, were run to ground at the Forest of Jardes. Bassus threw a cavalry cordon round the forest to prevent anyone escaping, and then sent in the infantry. The Jews attempted to break out by launching a series of attacks on the Roman lines, but each one was repulsed. After a lengthy fight the entire force was wiped out.

The Herodium was built by Herod the Great to cover the southern approaches to Jerusalem. According to recent archaeological surveys, this pseudo-volcanic structure also contains his mausoleum. (Bibleplaces.com)

The fortress of Machaerus, viewed from its only approach road to the south-east. This isolated redoubt (where John the Baptist had been imprisoned and beheaded) capitulated when a leader among the garrison was captured during a sortie and threatened with crucifixion. (Bibleplaces.com)

LEFT
The forbidding heights of Masada. The great plateau on the top of this rock-cut fortress measures 600m north–south and 300m east–west at its widest point, and is almost entirely circled by cliffs. Along part of the eastern side there is a 400m sheer drop, and from this side the only way to reach the top is by a precipitous, winding single-lane path known from antiquity as the snake path. (Author's Collection)

RIGHT
There are two large and six small Roman camps encircling Masada. The large ones are B in the east and F in the west, each measuring approximately 135m by 155m. The main strength of *legio X Fretensis* (numbering about 5,000 men) is believed to have been housed in these two camps. The six smaller camps apparently housed auxiliary troops. (Livius.org)

When Bassus suddenly died, the command, and the responsibility for exterminating the last remaining Jews outside of Roman authority, passed to Flavius Silva. The ensuing siege of Masada and the death before dishonour resolution of the Sicarii holdouts there is popularly interpreted as the last stand of a defiant Jewish nation. Ironically, the Sicarii never recognized the authority of any regime in Jerusalem and would have fought any bid to integrate them within the Jewish republic that stumbled into being in AD 66 as fiercely as they did against Rome. After seizing Masada at the outset of the revolt the contribution of the Sicarii to the Jewish war effort was nil. Far from taking the field against Rome, they spent the next five years raiding and plundering every village within reach of their citadel, reducing the entire area to a desert. This total indifference to the lives, property and customs of their own people reached its climax one Passover when they stormed the town of Ein-Gedi, killing 700 Jewish women and children after their men had fled, looting the houses and carrying off the crops.

There were close to a thousand holdouts living on top of the great, flat rock of Masada when the Romans finally arrived in the winter of AD 73. In addition to the Sicarii there were refugees from Qumran, Jerusalem and other desolated places. There were women as well as men, and there were

TOP

Camp F, which is located by the foot of the siege ramp on the north-western side of Masada, manifests the classic layout of a Roman military camp. Its dry stone walls, which originally stood about 3m high, enclosed a roughly rectangular area. Four gates, one on each side, gave access to the two main roads inside the camp. Note the smaller camp (F2) in the south-west corner, which was occupied briefly by a garrison after the fall of Masada. (Author's Collection)

MIDDLE

The Roman siege wall extending around Masada. Based on the size of the camps, the total number of soldiers who participated in the siege is estimated at about 8,000 to 9,000. (Bibleplaces.com)

BOTTOM

Flavius Silva ordered construction of a ramp to ascend the line of this natural spur, the White Rock (Leuke), in order to bring his siege equipment to bear against the defensive wall. (Author's Collection)

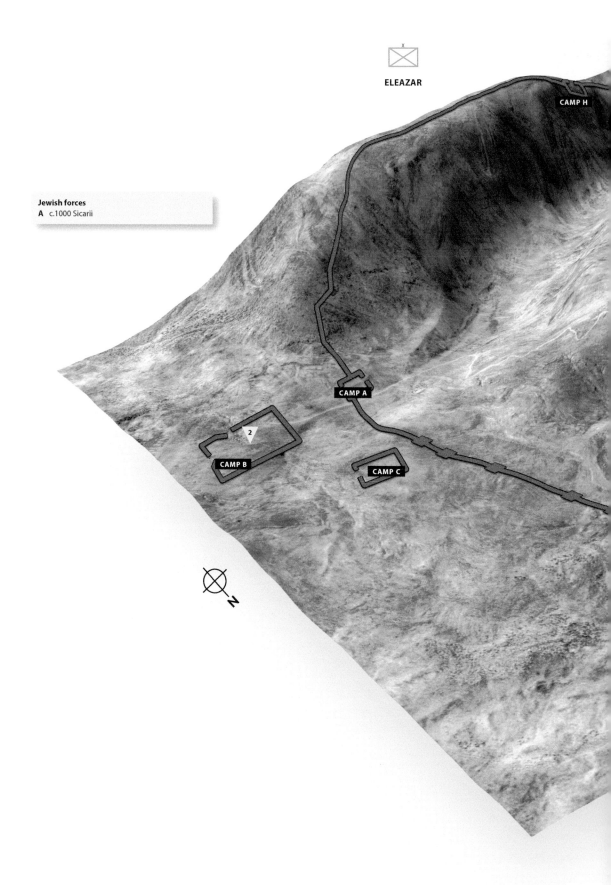

ELEAZAR

CAMP H

CAMP A

CAMP B

2

CAMP C

Jewish forces
A c.1000 Sicarii

N

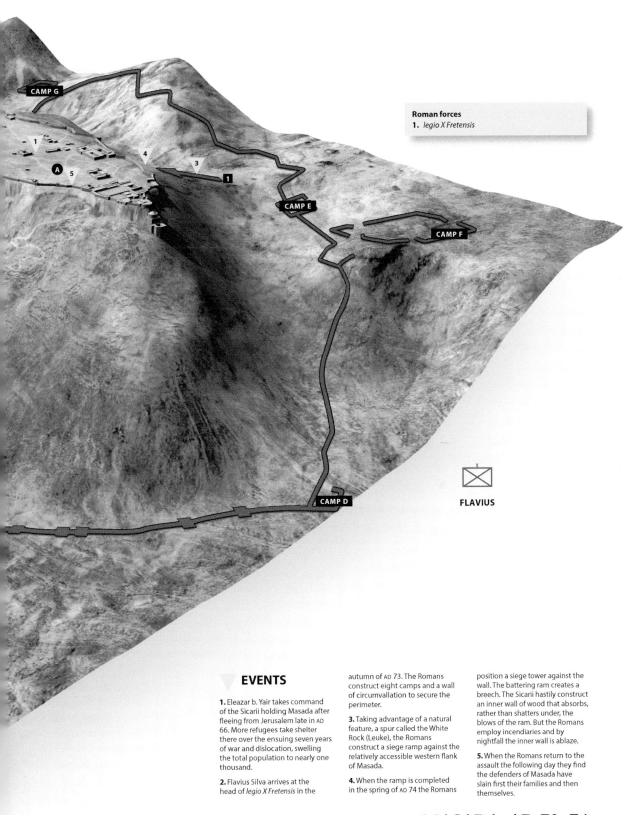

CAMP G

Roman forces
1. legio X Fretensis

CAMP E

CAMP F

CAMP D

FLAVIUS

▼ EVENTS

1. Eleazar b. Yair takes command of the Sicarii holding Masada after fleeing from Jerusalem late in AD 66. More refugees take shelter there over the ensuing seven years of war and dislocation, swelling the total population to nearly one thousand.

2. Flavius Silva arrives at the head of *legio X Fretensis* in the autumn of AD 73. The Romans construct eight camps and a wall of circumvallation to secure the perimeter.

3. Taking advantage of a natural feature, a spur called the White Rock (Leuke), the Romans construct a siege ramp against the relatively accessible western flank of Masada.

4. When the ramp is completed in the spring of AD 74 the Romans position a siege tower against the wall. The battering ram creates a breech. The Sicarii hastily construct an inner wall of wood that absorbs, rather than shatters under, the blows of the ram. But the Romans employ incendiaries and by nightfall the inner wall is ablaze.

5. When the Romans return to the assault the following day they find the defenders of Masada have slain first their families and then themselves.

MASADA, AD 73–74
The final Jewish stronghold is overcome.

The reconstructed base of the Roman siege tower deployed at Masada. The structure would have been built to the same template as the towers utilized against Jerusalem. (Bibleplaces. com)

children, a number of whom had no doubt been born on Masada and had never set foot in the world below. There were large stockpiles of weapons and food in the fortress, and a plentiful supply of water; Herod had constructed huge cisterns and a system of dams and aqueducts to fill them during the rainy season.

A more impregnable position is hard to imagine. Conversely, once the Roman siege lines had been established, the Sicarii weren't going anywhere, either, and with no prospect of help from the outside, their fate was sealed. Inexorably, the Romans constructed a ramp to scale the heights, and when it reached the level of the plateau, the assault began. Such combat as there was lasted only one day. By nightfall, the first defensive wall had been breached and the second was in flames.

Aware the end was nigh, Eleazar b. Yair, in the speech invented for him by Josephus, exhorted his fighters to embrace annihilation: 'let us go out of the world, together with our children and our wives, in a state of freedom.' Such an action, he added, without quoting any precedent, 'is that our laws command us to do', and, without asking their opinion, 'is what our wives and children crave at our hands'. Most importantly, 'God himself hath brought this necessity upon us.'

A handful of Sicarii remained at large after the fall of Masada, although not in Judea. They sought to rouse the diaspora communities in Alexandria and Cyrenaica against Rome, but were sold out to imperial authority and liquidated in short order.

LATER CONFRONTATIONS: THE KITOS WAR

LEFT
Boulders stockpiled at Masada for the use of the garrison in dropping on, or rolling at, the besiegers. (Bibleplaces.com)

RIGHT
Missile weapons collected at Masada, ranging from sling stones to ballista shot. (Author's Collection)

The terms of the *Pax Romana* forced on those surviving Jews in the aftermath of their defeat were harsh. The Temple was not to be rebuilt, and the High Priesthood and the Sanhedrin were abolished. Prior to the war the levy paid for the Temple had been the responsibility of adult men between the ages of 20 and 50 and living in Judea only. In the aftermath, the *Fiscus Iudaicus* was imposed on all Jews, including women, children and the elderly, wherever they lived in the Empire, and went straight to the Roman treasury. Only those who abandoned Judaism were exempt from paying it. Worst of all, the Jews found themselves dispossessed in their own country. With most of Judea now under direct Roman rule, henceforth the peasants would be tenants of the Emperor. Jewish disaffection would boil over, ironically not at a moment of Roman weakness but rather as the Empire reached the absolute floodtide of its supremacy.

In AD 113 the Parthian King Osroes I, who was in the midst of an internal struggle with a rival, Vologases III, for the throne, sought to strengthen his position by deposing the king of Armenia and replacing him with his nephew. The Roman response was immediate. The Emperor Trajan marched into Armenia the following year and annexed the entire kingdom as a Roman province.

Over the following two years, Trajan pushed south from Armenia directly into Parthian territory. Assyria and Mesopotamia – including the Parthian capital of Ctesiphon – were annexed and the Emperor was awarded the honorific *Parthicus*. The inexorable Roman advance culminated in Charax on the shore of the Persian Gulf in AD 116.

Trajan was now musing aloud about following in the footsteps of Alexander. But in reality the Roman frontier was already grossly overextended. Osroes remained at large, and now everywhere along a front 1,000km long the Parthians were able to harass the invader from the foothills east of the Tigris. Roman supply lines were dangerously exposed, and the fortress of Hatra, bypassed by the legions, became a focus of resistance.

There were an estimated one million Jews residing in Mesopotamia at this time, and they aggressively participated in the agitation against the Roman occupation. Of equal concern to Rome was the tenuous loyalty of those Jews within the Empire proper. The Parthian campaign denuded the eastern provinces of any but a token occupation force, since, besides the commitment of the five legions redeployed from Syria, Judea, Egypt and Cyrenaica, several cohorts were scrounged up from those left in order to augment the invasion force.

The Roman East, AD 74–136

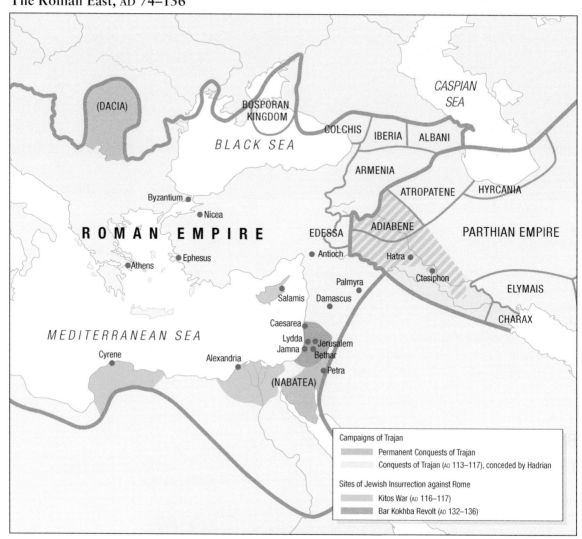

Inscription commemorating the conflict in Cyrenaica during the Kitos War. Orosius records the province was so depopulated new colonies had to be established by Hadrian: 'The Jews ... waged war on the inhabitants throughout Libya in the most savage fashion, and to such an extent was the country wasted that its cultivators having been slain, its land would have remained utterly depopulated, had not the Emperor Hadrian gathered settlers from other places and sent them thither, for the inhabitants had been wiped out.' (Livius.org)

Now that Parthia, the missing piece of the equation from AD 66–70, was involved in the general struggle against Rome, and perhaps interpreting a major earthquake that struck Syria in December AD 115 as the signal that the redemption of *Eretz Yisrael*, the Land of Israel, was nigh, Jewish insurrectionaries erupted in violence.

In Cyprus, Jewish rebels led by a local messianic pretender, Artemion, captured and sacked the city of Salamis, slaughtering its Greek population. Cassius Dio states that after the suppression of the revolt Jews were forbidden to settle on the island on pain of death.

This sestertius, minted near the end of Trajan's reign, depicts the Emperor ascendant over subjected figures representing Armenia, the Euphrates and the Tigris. The Empire achieved its greatest geographical extent during Trajan's reign; in addition to the territories portrayed, Dacia and Nabatea were also absorbed within the Roman orbit. (Classical Numismatic Group, http://cngcoins.com/)

Another messianic leader, called Lukuas by Eusebius, seized control of, and laid waste to, Cyrenaica. Lukuas then moved on Egypt and seized Alexandria, destroying pagan temples and the tomb of the hated Pompey.

In order to quell these serious disturbances, Trajan committed forces under Lusius Quietus, the commander of his Mauritanian auxiliaries. Lukuas was run to ground attempting to inspire revolt in Judea, but this was suppressed when the Jewish freedom fighters under the brothers Julian and Pappus were besieged in Lydda and wiped out. Quietus was appointed governor of Judea, where he was responsible for a forced policy of Hellenization; in response, according to the Mishnah, the rabbis ordered Jewish fathers not to teach their sons Greek.

THE FINAL CONFRONTATION: BAR KOKHBA'S REVOLT

Trajan's successor Hadrian rationalized the frontiers by withdrawing from Mesopotamia. His policy of Romanization, which included a ban on circumcision and laying the foundation of a pagan city, Aelia Capitolina, on the ruins of Jerusalem sparked the greatest, and final, war with the Jews.

This was no spontaneous uprising as had left the Jews almost accidentally in possession of their independence in AD 66. This time the Jewish revolt was premeditated and directed by a single leader. To judge by his battle cry – 'All we ask, oh Lord, is: Do not aid the enemy. Us, you need not help!' – his character was more iconoclastic than holy. But he was recognized as the messiah by Rabbi Akiva b. Joseph, the authoritative religious voice of the Jews in this age, and is known to history as Simon Bar Kokhba, 'Son of the Star'.

Another sestertius of Trajan, featuring the Emperor interacting with the human foundation of imperial power; the army. He is depicted seated on a platform, flanked by two officers, addressing and receiving the acclamation of his legions. (Classical Numismatic Group, http://cngcoins.com/)

Having spent years stockpiling weapons and constructing a network of communication tunnels and concealed redoubts that honeycombed the province, the Jews rose up in AD 132 and established a sovereign and independent state. Coins were struck, a new High Priest was elected and legal documents signed by Bar Kokhba as the *Nasi Israel* (Prince of Israel) show that Roman imperial estates were confiscated and leased out to Jewish peasants. Bar Kokhba's headquarters, which housed the Sanhedrin, was near

Jerusalem at Bethar, a strategic location on a mountain ridge overlooking both the Valley of Sorek and the important Jerusalem–Bet Guvrin Road.

Rome's local field commanders were outmatched; Hadrian was forced to dispatch enormous reinforcements under the governor of Britain, Sextus Julius Severus. Four legions were deployed – *VI Ferrata*, *X Fretensis*, *II Traiana Fortis* and *XXII Deiotariana* – and no less than 17 auxiliary units are known to have fought in Judea, including units borrowed from *II Cyrenaica*, *III Gallica* and *IV Scythica*. It is indicative of the ferocity of the campaign that *legio XXII Deiotariana* was so decimated during this conflict it was probably dissolved, since there are no indications of its subsequent existence. 'Many Romans, moreover, perished in this war', Cassius Dio conceded, noting that Hadrian, in writing to the Senate in its aftermath, did not employ the traditional salutation, 'If you and your children are in health, it is well; I and the army are in health.'

Ctesiphon, on the banks of the Tigris, was established as their capital by the Parthians. Its proximity to the frontier made it vulnerable. Trajan's occupation of the city in AD 117 was the first of five occasions it would be taken by the Romans. The great arch, all that remains of the palace complex today, was erected under the successor Sassanian dynasty. (Jamesdale10 via Wikipedia)

By the peak of the campaign Rome had committed the equivalent of 12 legions to suppress the revolt.

In AD 135, Hadrian's army besieged Bethar and on the 9th of Av (likely a traditional, rather than a genuine, date), the Jewish fast day commemorating the destruction of the first and second Holy Temples, the walls of Bethar fell. After a fierce battle, every Jew in Bethar was killed; according to Talmudic sources, the Romans 'went on killing until their horses were submerged in blood to their nostrils'.

In the account of Cassius Dio, 50 of the most important Jewish strongholds and 985 of the better-known villages were razed to the ground. A total of 580,000 Jews were killed in the various engagements or battles alone; whether or not this figure includes non-combatants, such as those children wrapped in Torah scrolls by the Romans and set alight, is uncertain.

A coin of the Bar Kokhba republic in Judea. Its appeal to Jewish tradition is encapsulated in its iconography – on the obverse, the Temple façade, with the Ark of the Covenant within and a star (Bar Kokhba's symbol) above. On the reverse is the simple legend, 'For the freedom of Jerusalem', surrounding a lulav with etrog. (Classical Numismatic Group, http://cngcoins.com/)

This coin celebrates 'Year 2 of the freedom of Israel' and is testament to the success of Bar Kochba in establishing a unitary Jewish state. The currency of the Bar Kokhba republic was not minted but rather over-stamped on top of existing Roman coins. (Classical Numismatic Group, http://cngcoins.com/)

LEGACY

As a result of her struggle with Rome, Israeli independence was definitively lost and the Jewish state disappeared from the map for more than 1,800 years. Many of those Jews not sold into slavery fled or were exiled abroad, marking this as the definitive origin of the diaspora.

Jerusalem, too, went into eclipse. Jews were forbidden to live in Aelia Capitolina, and were permitted to enter the city only once a year, on the 9th of Av, to mourn their losses. A Temple to Jupiter was constructed on the site of Herod's Temple. Not only did the Jews lose title to their city; Rome sought to strip their entire heritage from history. The Gezeirah, the Age of the Decree, circumcision, the Sabbath and the teaching of the Torah were all forbidden, and Hadrian ordered the name of the province changed from Judea to Syria Palaestina. This could, perhaps, be interpreted as the ultimate tribute to Jewish tenacity; never before (or after) was a province renamed as a corollary of a revolt against Rome.

The Jewish wars had other, long-term implications that went far beyond the immediate struggles over status and territory. Christian and Jewish scholars alike point out the rebellion as the final parting of the ways between the followers of Jesus, until then a dissident sect of Judaism, and the Pharisaic-rabbinical tradition of mainstream Judaism.

This coin, another in the 'For the freedom of Jerusalem' series, features a bunch of grapes on the obverse and a lyre with three strings on the reverse. (Classical Numismatic Group, http://cngcoins.com/)

THE BATTLEFIELD TODAY

The Holy Land remains as heavily trafficked – and bitterly contested – today as it was during the Jewish Revolt. Accordingly, planning a staff ride is both the easiest and chanciest of propositions for the military historian. Tour companies catering to the needs of pilgrims from three great faiths crisscross practically every square inch of the modern state of Israel, so booking an itinerary, guide, transport and accommodation can be arranged from anywhere on Earth within hours. Alternatively, you can just fly in, pick up a rental car and strike out on your own; in Israel, all roads lead to the site of a battle, siege or single combat.

A good place to start exploring Jerusalem is at the Israel Museum with the scale model of the city as it was on the eve of the war. Other period highlights include the Burnt House, the nearby Wohl Archaeological Museum and the Tower of David Museum.

Although the contours of Herod's city remain intact, the attentions of the Romans in AD 70 and the intervening centuries of occupation by great powers of other faiths means nothing remains of his Temple. The Temple

A watchtower at Masada. Along with the Sicarii, many Essenes took refuge here after their own settlement at Qumran was sacked by the legions. The Essenes War Scroll foretold the ultimate doom of Rome: 'The dominion of the Kittim shall come to an end and iniquity shall be vanquished, leaving no remnant; for the Sons of Darkness there shall be no escape.' (Author's Collection)

The synagogue at Masada. This may have been the spot where Eleazar b. Yair's men cast lots to determine the order by which they would turn their weapons on each other. (Author's Collection)

Mount (Haram al-Sharif) is accessible for non-Muslims during restricted hours, but advance permission is required for entry into the Dome of the Rock or the Al-Aqsa Mosque. The perspective gazing east across the Kidron Valley towards the Mount of Olives has changed little over the intervening near-two millennia since the *legio X Fretensis* was stationed there. On the opposite side of the structure, standing at the base of the famous Wailing Wall will enable the visitor to appreciate the monumental scale of the Temple Mount's masonry and the challenge its heights presented to the besiegers. All that is left otherwise is rubble, although ongoing excavations have restored much of the exterior of the Temple Mount at its base on the southern side, and recent digs have begun to reveal the warren of tunnels networking its interior.

Most of the other sites associated with the war are accessible as day-trips from Jerusalem. There is much history to soak up on a drive parallel to the coast or around the Sea of Galilee. Other highlights include the ruins of Gamala and the still impressive fortifications of Machaerus and the Herodium. No tour would be complete without visiting Masada. Towering over the Dead Sea, the restored site of the last stand comes complete with a museum displaying artifacts from the siege and a cable car that whisks sightseers up and down the steep slopes. From the heights, with their panoramic view of the surrounding Roman camps and fieldworks, perfectly preserved by the desert's aridity and heat, visitors can easily imagine themselves in the place of the Sicarii, watching the noose inexorably tighten.

Of course, all of the above can be rendered meaningless overnight by the ever-turbulent nature of politics, domestic and international, in the Holy Land. Ironically, having your carefully prepackaged vacation spiked without warning by the violence unleashed during one of the region's periodic eruptions of religious-nationalist messianic idealism might be the best way to put yourself in the place of a tourist circa AD 66.

BIBLIOGRAPHY

Our primary source for events in Judea leading up to, and during, the war with Rome is of course Flavius Josephus. His bold claim that 'I wrote my history of the war being a participant in many of the events, and [as] an eyewitness to most of them, I was ignorant of nothing that was either said or done', cannot be matched by any other author in antiquity, but we can glean additional information from Suetonius, Tacitus, Cassius Dio, The New Testament and the Rabbinical tradition of the Torah and Mishnah. Modern studies of the archaeological, epigraphic and numismatic evidence help us flesh out this picture. Useful secondary sources include, but are not limited to:

Aberbach, Moshe, and Aberbach, David, *The Roman-Jewish Wars and Hebrew Cultural Nationalism* St. Martin's Press: New York, 2000

Berlin, Andrea M., and Overman, J. Andrew (eds.), *The First Jewish Revolt: Archaeology, History, and Ideology*, Routledge, London (2002)

Bloom, James J., *The Jewish Revolts against Rome, A.D. 66–135: A Military Analysis*, McFarland & Co., Jefferson (2010)

Brauer, George C., Jr., *Judea Weeping: The Jewish Struggle against Rome from Pompey to Masada, 63 B.C. to A.D. 73*, Crowell, New York (1970)

Brighton, Mark Andrew, *The Sicarii in Josephus's Judean War: Rhetorical Analysis and Historical Observations* Society of Biblical Literature: Atlanta, 2009

Curran, John R., 'The Jewish War: Some Neglected Regional Factors', *Classical World*, Vol. 101, No. 1 (2007), pp. 75–91

Eck, Werner, 'The Bar Kokhba Revolt: the Roman point of view', *The Journal of Roman Studies*, Vol. 89, 1999, pp. 76–89

Faulkner, Neil, *Apocalypse: The Great Jewish Revolt Against Rome*, Tempus Publishing, New York (2004)

Furneaux, Rupert, *The Roman Siege of Jerusalem*, Hart-Davis MacGibben, London (1973)

Goodman, Martin, *The Ruling Class of Judea: The Origins of the Jewish Revolt against Rome A.D. 66–70*, Cambridge University Press, Cambridge (1987)

Price, Jonathan J., *Jerusalem Under Siege: The Collapse of the Jewish State*, 66–70 C.E., Brill, New York (1992)

Reznick, Leibel, *The Mystery of Bar Kokhba: An Historical and Theological Investigation of the Last King of the Jews* J. Aronson: Northvale, NJ, 1996

Roth, C., 'The Constitution of the Jewish Republic of 66–70', *Journal of Jewish Studies*, Vol. 9 (1964), pp. 295–319

Roth, Jonathan, *The Logistics of the Roman Army in the Jewish War*, Ph.D. Dissertation, Columbia University (1991)

Schäfer, Peter (ed.), *The Bar Kokhba War Reconsidered: New Perspectives on the Second Jewish Revolt against Rome* Mohr Siebeck: Tübingen, 2003

Shargel, Baila R.; 'The Evolution of the Masada Myth', Judaism, 28, 1979, pp. 357–71

Seward, Desmond, *Jerusalem's Traitor: Josephus, Masada, and the Fall of Judea*, Da Capo Press, Cambridge (2009)

Smallwood, E. Mary, *The Jews under Roman Rule: from Pompey to Diocletian*, Brill, Leiden (2001)

Sorek, Susan, *The Jews against Rome*, Continuum, New York (2008)

INDEX